Saving Graces

reflections on hope
in everyday life

Bertha Catherine Madott

© 2000 Novalis, Saint Paul University, Ottawa, Canada

Cover: Blair Turner
Layout: Cynthia F. Roy

Novalis, Saint Paul University
223 Main Street
Ottawa, Ontario, Canada
K1S 1C4

Canadian Cataloguing in Publication Data

Madott, Bertha Catherine, 1948–
    Saving graces: reflections on hope in everyday life

ISBN 2-89507-073-3

    1. Spiritual life. I. Title.

BV4517.M33 2000   248   C99-901692-X

Printed in Canada.

We acknowledge the financial support of the Government of Canada through the Book Publishing Industry Development Program (BPIDP) for our publishing activities.

Dedication

In memory of my grandmothers,
Donna Pasquale and Caterina Madott,
two inspiring examples of
courage, endurance and hope.

Contents

Work

Play

Simple Comforts

Hope

Joy

Glad Tidings: An Introduction

Where do books come from? I can't speak for others, but my inspiration usually begins with a question. How can I explore a theme that somehow eluded my grasp in the past? A few years ago, the human yearning for pleasure, satisfaction and hope captured my attention. This book is the result of my search for answers.

The experiences recorded here were not shaped by naive optimism. As I wrote and reflected, I experienced the usual ups and downs of life: a splendid family wedding followed by a tragic funeral; a frustrating new computer system at work; a delightful weekend getaway with my husband; a painful back problem; a capable doctor's reassuring care. And yet, in spite of the shadows of struggle and sadness, my thoughts and feelings always returned to the sunshine.

This book reflects my personal experience of the Divine Presence in the fabric of the most ordinary events. Every story recounted in these pages is true. I have changed some names and details to protect the privacy of those concerned and, in a few cases, I have telescoped events for the sake of brevity. But these hopeful, joyful stories are not sanitized or fictionalized escapes into wishful thinking: they are living witnesses to the existence of Grace.

Two of the four Gospels begin the story of Jesus' life right from his birth in simple, ordinary, even humble circumstances. Two thousand years later, they invite us to experience the continuing presence of God in our midst through the most humble, ordinary and simple incidents of every day. In my case, these are events in the life of a self-employed fifty-something woman, living in a large city.

God's heart overflows like a fountain, pouring graces of every kind onto creation. This little book will describe the everyday blessings which sustain me through good times and bad. May these reflections help you to find comfort and joy in the ordinary events of your own unique, rich and precious life.

Young

Duet

Show and Tell

One Door Closes, Another Door Opens

Out of the Mouths of Babes

Legacy

Awakening

Grace before Meals

Duet

"What's the matter with kids today?" These cranky, middle-aged words sprang to my lips as I surveyed the latest vandalism of the bank machine near my local subway station. The damage? A chocolate ice cream cone smashed into a computer screen. Sticky red syrup dripping down the counter. Grubby yellow popcorn ground into the tile floor. The bank technician cleaning up the mess joined me in lamenting the state of the world. He told me that Head Office was fed up with our destructive local teenagers. After this latest "incident" was "resolved," the bank machine would be removed, not repaired.

By Sunday, I had forgotten all about vandals and bank machines, until I saw the boarded-up corner beside the subway while walking to church. The plywood barrier provided a troubling reminder of the generation gap. In spite of the cheerful blue sky above me, my thoughts turned glum and grey.

At church it was my turn to be lector, so I contributed my readings from scripture and then sat in a pew near the altar. I was dimly aware of someone behind me – Mary Catherine, one of our most faithful altar servers.

Eventually it was time for communion. Up in the choir loft the soloist, a real live opera singer, began to sing a modern hymn. But I thought I could hear another voice nearby, the voice of someone other than the soloist. I soon realized that my companion, Mary Catherine the altar server, was singing. Oblivious to my presence, she sang without reservations, without embarrassment, without fear. Also without any music. I know because I peeked.

Had she learned this song in school, from a recording, or at music lessons? Did she have secret youthful dreams about sharing her talents with others in public, just as our resident opera singer did? Or did she sing simply for the joy of it? I'll probably never know.

But to my great happiness, some irresistible impulse moved the altar girl to sing quietly along with the soloist, in a voice audible only to a person sitting nearby. For a few moments, the two voices together, the confident operatic soprano and the soft teenage treble, created a memorable duet. And I learned an unforgettable lesson about the creative gifts that young people can share with this world.

O Lord of schoolgirls and opera singers, thank you for letting me hear the clear note of faith in Mary Catherine's fresh, youthful voice.

Show and Tell

One evening, just as we were about to put supper on the table, the doorbell rang and there stood Erik, our 14-year-old neighbour. "I have something special to show you," he said with a grin. I put the plates in the oven to keep warm, while Erik marched straight into the living room, carrying a bulky green garbage bag. He began removing the contents right in the middle of our hardwood floor.

Erik proceeded to assemble a complicated arrangement of straws, plastic tubing, construction paper and cardboard, talking and gesturing in great excitement. He was, he said, building a space station. With moveable parts. A landing dock. A hydraulic arm.

He had taken part in a science fair project and his team had been chosen to go to the province-wide finals. On the day of the competition, he and his buddies faced a compulsory construction problem. Working to a strict deadline, and using specific materials, they had to build a space station capable of performing certain mechanical functions. The contraption on the living room floor was their answer to the challenge. And it had won the team a prize!

Erik and his space station showed me a different facet of teenage life today. I knew he played drums in the band and I'd seen him whizzing down the streets on his mountain bike. But, as he eagerly explained, the winter months spent on his school projects had taught him to solve complex math and science problems, while working creatively with others.

Erik and his teammates enjoyed challenges that would baffle some of their elders (especially techno-dunces like me).

Erik's demonstration encouraged me to relax about the future of society. After all, I had personally witnessed one of our future engineers happily at work on my living room floor, creating a scientific miracle using straws, plastic tubing, construction paper and cardboard.

O Lord of science and technology, I am inspired – and reassured – by the enthusiasm and imagination of teenagers like Erik: drummer, biker, engineer-in-training.

One Door Closes, Another Door Opens

Another funeral, the fifth one since January. I sat down in the pew with rather a poor grace, thinking of what was to come: the tears of my relatives, unhappy memories, a sombre eulogy. Alas. My patience with the ebbs and flows of life was definitely at low tide.

As I waited for the funeral procession to begin, what should catch my eye but a small booklet, tucked behind the hymn books. It turned out to be a beautiful little pamphlet prepared for a First Communion celebration held in the church just the day before.

For fifteen blessed minutes, I read and re-read the little pamphlet, forgetting all about the impending funeral. Letting my imagination wander, I saw in my mind's eye a different procession coming into the church, led by the young boys and girls listed in the pamphlet. Here was Amanda, looking just like a princess in her special white dress. Behind her walked Mom and Dad, a brother and sister, assorted other relatives, all dressed in spring clothes – elegant flowered hats, sprightly silk ties – not a black outfit in sight.

Because the little booklet carefully listed the participants, it was easy to imagine the friends who sang in the choir, the altar servers who assisted the parish priest, the sick relatives who couldn't attend, the other kids who celebrated birthdays around this time.

I read with amusement the names of all the children making their first communion, names popular for little girls today. Ashley, Tiffany, Jennifer and others all had their part in the ceremony. I savoured the little prayer for children attributed to Mother Teresa. I enjoyed every word of another child's "thank you message" to those who helped make her day so special. Even the typing mistakes made me smile.

And then, all too soon, the funeral began. Putting my daydream aside, I picked up a hymn book and let my voice join all the others. Tears came to my eyes as I saw my cousin and his family stoically follow the coffin up the aisle. Another funeral, the fifth one since January! Alas.

At the Gospel, I heard Jesus' inspiring words commending me to be "childlike in spirit." And, in spite of the grief surrounding me, I thought of Amanda and Ashley, Tiffany and Jennifer, all in their pretty white dresses, and once again I smiled.

During a time of sadness, my imagination was brightened by the thought of happy young girls in white dresses. Thank you, Lord.

Out of the Mouths of Babes

Saturday afternoon, my last day at music camp. Turning up my nose at the schedule of events, I decided to spend my time cleaning out the tent and packing up the car instead. My friends were shocked at these plans. "What! You're not coming to the children's concert?" they exclaimed. Swayed by their enthusiasm, I followed them down to the recital hall.

My recollections of children's concerts 40 years ago include crying students, nail-biting parents and stern-voiced music teachers. Kids sometimes fainted from sheer terror! But this concert proved to be completely different.

First up on the stage were the absolute beginners, mostly four-year-olds. Cymbals, drums, specially tuned xylophones, triangles: someone very different from the stern-voiced music teachers of long ago had obviously organized this class. And the students? They seemed considerably less anxious about performing in public than I ever did. All of them smiled. Most of them seemed to be having fun. And if they got lost, there was the gently smiling teacher, whispering encouragement from the sidelines.

After the absolute beginners came a group with considerably more experience. These performers were six years old. They played something on the recorder using grown-up sheet music. Another smiling teacher, also whispering encouragement, shepherded them safely around any treacherous musical land-mines. These youngsters had been little more than absolute beginners on Monday morning. Now, Saturday afternoon, they had just played a simple piece in public. The applause was tumultuous.

And so it went. A duo of 10-year-old boys, scowling from the ferocity of their concentration. A string quartet of elegant pre-teens. A few choral groups, one singing a hand-clapping, foot-stomping Gospel number. A blond angel who stood up with his violin and announced with dignity, "I am now going to play a piece I wrote myself." Perhaps he was 12.

The afternoon passed all too quickly. Music was lost; music was found. Parents took videos. Children waved at cameras. Staff members calmed a few timid kids suffering from stage fright and the audience applauded their bravery. No one cried. Except me.

O God of celestial harmony, when next I'm called upon to make a joyful noise unto the Lord, remind me of the children's concert at music camp.

Legacy

"Such a tragedy," everyone said, "a man in the prime of life, so young and talented. A painter, sculptor, musician. An artist who loved to laugh, to work, to explore. Such a tragedy."

At the funeral home, the man's children, teenagers really, tried hard to put on a brave front. Rivers of tears flowed, and his children helped to dry some of them. Beside the coffin, on a simple easel, someone had placed a brilliant pencil sketch of the dead man. There he was, large as life, with his trademark beard and sunglasses, just as everyone remembered, laughing out loud at some outrageous joke. "When did he do this self-portrait?" visitors wondered. "Before he took sick in the winter?"

The answer to this ordinary question revealed the extraordinary legacy the artist had left to his children. For the drawing had been started in his hospital room by his youngest daughter, while her father lay quietly lost in the dreamland between life and death. She completed the sketch at home. When she finished her father's portrait, she joined her brothers and sister at work on a large canvas likewise intended as a parting gift to Dad. Together they painted a scene from the woods, with trees, sky, clouds, earth, just the sort of place their father loved, another fitting tribute from those who loved him.

The next day, when the funeral procession arrived at the old cemetery in the farm country near the family home, the funeral directors gently placed the children's canvas on top of the coffin. For a few minutes art and life came together: the green trees on the canvas juxtaposed against the brown wood of the casket, both set against the blue of an early spring sky, the southern tip of Lake Simcoe just visible in the distance.

A soft warm breeze came up as the mourners gathered for a few final prayers and tributes by the graveside. The painted cloth fluttered, threatening to blow away, until an alert attendant placed a floral arrangement of white roses and freesias on top, a gracious anchor.

Finally the service was officially over, and family and friends walked slowly back to their waiting cars. Those who turned around for one last look saw the coffin, decorated with blue sky, fir trees and roses, a beacon of love and hope, there on the top of the hill.

O Lord of the Resurrection, you too loved the sky and fields and hills. Teach me to see your beacon of love and hope even when my eyes are filled with tears.

Awakening

Lily took a job as a counsellor at Camp Awakening last summer when she was 16. One week she volunteered for a long canoe trip in Algonquin Park with six campers. Everyone slept in tents, struggled through portages and sang songs around the campfire, as people on canoe trips do. But there was one difference. Lily and the other staff members were counsellors to a group of girls with multiple handicaps: some were missing limbs, others needed walkers.

How in the world did these campers manage? Canoe trips, even at the best of times, are physically demanding endurance events. How did these brave girls survive, even flourish, for six days in the wilderness?

During the daily portages, the campers could barely carry one life jacket or paddle; the brunt of hauling the rest of the gear fell on the counsellors, all volunteers. In fact, the counsellors were on call around the clock for the whole six days, because the campers needed help eating and many were incontinent at night.

In between paddling canoes, pitching tents and making campsites, the young counsellors made some important discoveries. They learned to put their pity aside. The campers didn't feel sorry for themselves, so why should anyone else? Every little accomplishment filled the campers with the greatest satisfaction; the smiles on their faces helped Lily and her colleagues to accept the severe limitations of the group.

Eventually the counsellors learned to see the campers as real people, putting aside labels like "disabled" and "handicapped." And there on the waters of Algonquin Park, counsellors and campers alike experienced a tremendous awakening: life, they discovered, is precious for everyone, regardless of "ability."

O Lord of rushing waters, when I am frustrated by my own limitations, let me remember these brave girls, canoeing together in Algonquin Park.

Grace before Meals

Thanksgiving weekend, Sunday afternoon. I was the official chef, keeping an eye on the turkey that was roasting happily in the oven. Everyone else had gone outside to enjoy the fine fall weather. Everyone except me and William, one of our out-of-town visitors.

Earlier that afternoon, twelve-year-old William had looked pensively out the window. At that sensitive pre-teen stage, not sure if he wanted to be a kid or a grown-up, he suddenly seemed reluctant to play football with his younger brothers in the nearby park. He asked quietly, "Is it okay if I stay here with you instead?"

I replied in my most nonchalant voice. "Sure. I'm just working in the kitchen. Care to keep me company?" And to my surprise, William came in and pulled up a chair.

He sat, but not for long. One major job waited for someone's capable hands: the preparation of a tray of raw vegetables. William was mighty handy with a knife and chopping block: his aunt, a former chef, had taught him basic kitchen techniques. So I gave him the carrots, broccoli, cauliflower, radishes and peppers. And watched.

He started with the carrots, peeling, washing, slicing. I stayed as far in the background as my miniscule kitchen permitted. The only time I added my two cents' worth of adult advice was to insist that William clean up as he went along.

He carefully arranged the carrot sticks along the edge of an oval serving platter. Next he turned his attention to the radishes. And then the peppers. Little by little, he built up an attractive pattern of contrasting shapes, colours and textures with his expertly cut vegetables. (William had obviously taken his aunt's lessons to heart!) We needed my larger, stronger hands only once, to tackle an awkward giant cauliflower. Otherwise, William did everything himself.

Eventually the football players returned, other guests arrived, and the turkey emerged golden brown from the oven. We sat down to the usual Thanksgiving feast, and in the excitement of entertaining a crowd on a special day, I didn't think very much more about William in the kitchen. But later on, when the house was quiet, I recorded the dinner menu in a leather-bound guest book, a journal for memories of special meals with friends. I listed the dishes that I had cooked, all standard holiday fare: "Turkey, Cranberry Compote, Mashed Potatoes, Sage and Onion Stuffing." Then I added a note about the vegetable platter.

Next morning after breakfast, our guests prepared to leave. Distracted by all the hustle and bustle, I almost forgot to ask William and his brothers to autograph our guest book. The younger boys signed at the bottom of the page, with the wobbly tentative handwriting of children. Then it was William's turn.

My kitchen helper read the menu and a smile lit up his face when he noticed *William's Raw Vegetables*, written there for all the world to see, a milestone in his personal culinary history. It was a milestone for me, too: a reminder of how blessed I am when I treasure the gifts of my youngest friends.

Happy Thanksgiving, William! Do you think your mom should let you carve the Hallowe'en pumpkin this year?

I am blessed, O Lord, by these your gifts, not just of bountiful food, but of young hands to help me in the kitchen.

Old

Riding on a Camel

My grandmother was a remarkable woman. The eldest of 13 children in a poor immigrant family, she triumphed over a deprived, even abusive childhood. She grew into a much-loved and respected symbol of strength, energy and enthusiasm, not just to her family, but to hundreds of friends around the world. Of all her adventures, the one I love best concerns a camel in the Sinai desert.

Grannie loved to travel; my grandfather, on the other hand, was determined never to sleep away from home. So my grandmother resolved early in her married life to find more willing travel companions. These eventually included friends, various compliant relatives and even organized tour groups.

When she was 82, her church arranged a guided pilgrimage to Israel, to visit all the usual historic sites in Jerusalem, Bethlehem and Nazareth. The pious pilgrims could pray at the shrines, meditate on the beauty of the countryside and walk the same paths as Jesus and the patriarchs – standard fare in a tourist destination called "The Holy Land." Grannie was one of the first to sign up.

One bright sunny day, the tour took the pilgrims on a secular sight-seeing drive. There in the desert, especially organized for their entertainment, was a once-in-a-lifetime opportunity to ride on a real live camel. The bearded and swarthy camel drivers stood hopefully by the side of the road, camels a-ready, but this group, consisting of mostly elderly and middle-aged ladies, was far too dignified for such nonsense. Except for Grannie. Ashamed that none of her younger companions would accept the invitation of the "nice camel drivers," she said, "Why not?" and went forward.

Afterwards she reported that the camel was very large (she was barely five feet tall). It was not at all easy to climb onto the wooden seat, even though the camel was sitting down. Then once the camel stood up, how high they were! And how the camel swayed as he walked!

Someone had the wit to snap a picture of this incredible scene. There is Grannie, 82 years old, with white hair and bifocals, sitting atop a huge camel; her plump arms and legs look rather pink after a week in the desert sun. She is wearing one of her trademark sleeveless sweaters buttoned across a familiar floral dress, the dress pulled up well above her dimpled knees. The camel, as camels do, looks surly and mean. Grannie, however, is all smiles.

O Lord of the desert, when I'm frightened by the thought of growing old, remind me of Grannie and her ride on the camel. Thank you for the prospect of a lifetime of adventures.

How Many for Lunch Today?

My grandfather never really retired. In his late 60s he turned the reins of the family business over to his son, but "Poppy" still went into work almost every day. Even when he was over 80, he still had important duties in the office, things like opening and sorting the mountains of mail, and signing the payroll cheques. I helped him with the payroll as he sat in a big leather chair at his desk, and we worked companionably together for an hour or two. He was a wonderful example of how to grow old with strength and dignity.

Banking and payroll duties aside, in his later years my grandfather's contribution to running the business more often took place in the office kitchen, strategically located right next to the executive dining room. Poppy was an expert at preparing certain traditional "old country" recipes. These may have had their origins years ago in the farm kitchens of southern Italy, but they taste equally delicious served today in fancier surroundings. Once a week, Poppy would take over the kitchen right after the morning coffee break to create some simple but memorable meal. Eggs fried with hot peppers in olive oil, and pasta with *ceci* (chick peas) were two of his specialties. Both used simple ingredients but they required a master's touch to make them truly delicious.

As the morning went on, tantalizing aromas escaped from the kitchen every time the door opened, for Poppy had plenty of company while he cooked. Staff members, from senior sales managers to the most junior file clerks, came in to chat with the man whose official title once was "Chairman of the Board" but now might well have been "Grandfather at Large."

Poppy and his visitors discussed cooking techniques, the relative merits of different types of pasta, the quality of the current olive oil. Since the family business was in fact a food company, everything that went on in the kitchen could rightly be called "product research." As everyone knows, any worthwhile research in the food business necessarily involves cooking.

And then eating. Poppy prepared enough for a small army, planning to feed any of his family who were working that day (I was always there) plus anyone else who might be hungry. Who isn't hungry at lunchtime? At least 15 people regularly showed up to sample the results of Poppy's ongoing product research; there was always enough to go around.

I learned valuable lessons about office procedures signing the payroll cheques with Poppy. I learned about employee relations and the dignity of all labour there in the kitchen over a bowl of pasta and *ceci*.

O Lord of the harvest, I am grateful for what Poppy taught me in the office kitchen: everyone should be welcome at our table.

A Gardener's Prayer

In the autumn of her days, she waits patiently, hopefully, longingly for spring. At age 84, she doesn't expect miracles: bones creak and muscles ache, eyesight fades and memory is unreliable. But the garden is one miracle that never fails. When she was younger, she could do everything herself. Now she has to rely on others: a few helpful neighbours and her son. Love of gardening may be the most important bond they all share.

On an early spring day, one of the helpful neighbours rents a machine to till the hard ground; he digs his own garden then comes across the road to her land. Turning the earth is the first sign that the garden is coming back to life after the long winter. The son appears a day or two later with cow manure and peat moss, working the land once more. Meanwhile 100 tiny tomato seedlings are already flourishing indoors. She always starts her own plants in a sunny upstairs room, using seeds saved from the previous autumn. Now that she is alone in the house, there is plenty of space indoors for gardening projects. No overnight guests after the Christmas season, please, since all the spare beds are covered with trays of germinating seeds!

At the end of May the son, joking about filial duty, carries the tiny plants downstairs for his mother. She hovers nearby, getting in the way and offering unneeded advice. Perhaps they argue, but raised voices add spice to Mediterranean life and keep everyone's wits sharp. Too much peace can be like the grave sometimes. Then side by side they plant tomatoes all day.

Sometimes the mother, tired and stiff with arthritis, merely watches while the son works. Through July and August he comes over a couple of times a week to cut the grass, weed the flower beds, trim the hedges, fertilize the roses. They might disagree about where to prune the fruit trees, when to pick the pears, how to water the garden. But by the end of the summer, together, one way or another, they will have produced a staggering quantity of peaches and pears, zucchini and eggplant, but mostly tomatoes.

Come September, she will happily set to work canning the fruits of their combined labour. If, in her eyes, the crop is poor she will ask her son to bring over a few more bushels from the local farmers' market, and they will discuss what to buy and how much to spend. It is impossible for her to have too many tomatoes! Strangers might wonder why anyone 84 years old should be tending a garden of this size. A household of one, even with lots of guests, doesn't really need the dozens of jars that she preserves. But those who know better say that old habits die hard. The 100 tomato plants are a source of unfailing satisfaction, the garden the greatest pleasure she has left.

O Lord, I trust that you will watch me tend my garden through a lifetime of seasons, until I no longer need to feel the wind on my forehead, or the earth under my fingers.

Breaking Bread

We were happily enjoying a morning's drive through the countryside near my in-laws' farm in Southern Italy. Bewitched by the scenery, a new panorama waiting around every curve in the road, we ventured farther and farther off the beaten path, until finally we were, if not exactly lost, at least well removed from many signs of civilization.

We were heading, we hoped, in the direction of a 13th-century church. At last we arrived, to find the charming mediaeval structure now somewhat overgrown by vines and shrubbery and, alas, closed for the day. Oh well, we consoled ourselves, perhaps we could have a picnic lunch nearby, in the wonderful peace and beauty of the remote Italian countryside.

Picnic areas were as hard to find as road signs. Italians are not much given to lawns and grass, but there had to be some suitable spot close at hand. On our travels earlier in the day, we had with foresight stopped at an outdoor market to buy bread, olives and cheese, tomatoes and cucumbers. We never travelled without a Swiss army knife. Now all we needed was the space to enjoy these simple foods. Finally we stopped by a farmhouse to ask for suggestions. Was there anywhere nearby where we could spread out our little meal?

The old farmer, a perfect stranger to us, hardly needed a minute to think. He brushed away our request for directions to a "picnic spot" and instead invited us to sit with him at the chairs and tables outside his long, low farmhouse. He would provide the wine, he cheerfully suggested, as we had provided the food. For a makeshift tablecloth, we carefully ripped apart the paper bags holding our provisions; I cut the bread and cheese; our host brought out three tumblers and a flask of *vinello di campagna*, his simple homemade wine. We ate and drank our fill, talked about the trials of getting older, and eventually headed home, more than satisfied with our "picnic spot."

Even with the finest map, I doubt we could find the 13th-century church and the friendly farmer again. This region of Italy is blessed with an abundance of ancient churches as well as old men and long, low farmhouses. The guidebooks are no help either. I looked at a map just the other day; none of the place names seemed even the least bit familiar. In any case, how would you mark on a map, "Here you will find simple Christian charity"? That's what we found in the home of a generous old man who thought nothing of sharing his wine and breaking bread with strangers.

O Lord of old farmers and young tourists, our picnic at the farmhouse reminds me that you, too, broke the bread and blessed the wine with your friends.

The Red Rosary

The Rotunda was beautifully decorated. Guests stopped to admire the majestic long-stemmed calla lilies elegantly arranged in tall vases. The catering staff had outdone themselves, creating attractive displays of gleaming punch bowls and sparkling stemmed glasses. Chefs were still hard at work on the delicious party treats that would appear later: trays of fresh asparagus rolls, open-faced cucumber sandwiches and French pastries. Yet in spite of the gracious elegance of the Rotunda, we were not in the lobby of a fancy hotel, but in the entrance hall of Providence Centre, a senior citizens' residence. The festivities were in honour of the annual "Donor Recognition Day."

For me, however, the greatest pleasure of this special day was not found in the calla lilies and silver punch bowls, but in the sight of the residents, happily participating in the celebration. All of them were old, many very frail. Some of the residents arrived in mobile hospital beds complete with oxygen masks and intravenous drips; there were wheelchairs and walkers, braces and orthopedic supports of every kind. But regardless of their limitations and the assorted infirmities of old age, everyone wanted to attend the party.

The celebrations began with a Mass, and many of those gathering in the chapel arrived in wheelchairs. The offertory procession of residents was especially inspiring. One very frail woman, wheeled up the aisle by an attendant, clasped a cruet of wine in her gnarled fingers. A somewhat more mobile friend followed: in one hand she held the matching cruet of water while with the other hand she manipulated the controls on her electric wheelchair!

After Mass, I sat for a few minutes in my pew to reflect on what I had seen. My musings were interrupted by a perplexed elderly lady in a wheelchair, looking for a rosary she had left behind earlier in the morning. Together we hunted and eventually found it, exactly where she remembered leaving it, in a pew just a few feet away.

The lost rosary was made of red crystal beads, radiant as rubies. Aren't old ladies supposed to prefer insipid pastels? Perhaps this resident chose jewel colours because they were easier for fading eyes to find in a dim light. I would rather think she treasured her bright red rosary because, like the other guests at the party, she still wanted to enjoy life to the fullest: a life that included bright colours, gleaming punch bowls, fancy sandwiches and displays of beautiful flowers.

O Divine Providence, you have created us for an eternity of beauty and pleasure in your presence. Thank you for showing me that our need for joy has no age limits.

Noah's Flood: The Sequel

We left for vacation on a cold winter day. We returned three weeks later, on another cold winter day. From the outside, the house looked friendly and comfortable after our nights in a tent on a remote Mexican beach. But as soon as we walked in the door we knew that something was very wrong. Sure enough, a quick inspection revealed that some catastrophe had definitely taken place in the basement: boxes moved, a rug rolled up, rags piled beside the laundry tubs. Harry, the neighbour who had kept an eye on things during our trip, told us the whole horrible story.

Our basement had been seriously flooded. In a freak accident, the water meter had cracked, causing pipes to burst, a potential disaster in an empty house. Harry happily reassured us that on one of his daily inspection tours, he had spotted the rising waters (nearly a foot deep!), instantly called the city, had the meter repaired, and then cleaned up the mess. The only permanent damage was to the rug, a family cast-off that had seen better days, and one or two boxes of books.

Once the first shock had worn off (our humble home threatened by a flood!) we were almost overwhelmed with gratitude for all Harry's help. How could we possible repay him for everything he had done? Mindful of our manners and Harry's dignity, I quietly asked his wife if he would accept a bottle of something as a token of our appreciation. She brushed aside our concerns. She insisted that Harry was not at all put out by the catastrophe, saying gently but firmly, "You see, dearie, the flood was like an adventure. It gave him something to do."

For Harry, a healthy man in his mid-seventies, winters were long and boring. There wasn't enough to occupy him at home, no gardening, no lawn bowling, very few outings. Except for the Christmas season and the weekly curling match, not much happened between November, when the leaves had to be raked, and March, when spring clean-up time finally arrived. Our flood was the most interesting thing that had happened to poor Harry in several weeks!

It says in the Bible that Noah was 600 years old when the flood began. Perhaps that is why he so eagerly and faithfully followed the Lord's elaborate instructions for the construction of the ark. Like Harry many years later, Noah was still very much alive, alert and full of life. Retirement is altogether too boring for men like Noah and Harry; a good flood might be a welcome diversion, guaranteed to liven things up a little! All of us, age seven to 77, need to feel useful and appreciated. Thanks again, Harry, for saving our humble home.

O Lord of rising waters — whether caused by endless rain or broken pipes — thank you for the capable hands of the Noahs and Harrys of this world.

How Great Thou Art

On a beautiful May morning, an attractive, well-groomed woman sat quietly in a pew near the side door of the church. Wearing a dress and jacket printed all over with white and purple pansies, she was the very picture of spring. However, in spite of her softly waved brown hair, her delicate pink lipstick and the twinkle in her bright blue eyes, the lady of a certain age had passed the springtime of her youth. She was, in fact, somebody's grandmother.

The proof was there in the pew right beside her, in the presence of her daughter holding a new grandson. The young mother looked remarkably like the older woman: the same wavy brown hair, the same cheerful face. But where the older woman had laugh lines at the corners of her eyes and the beginnings of a double chin, her daughter's skin was still as fresh and flawless as the flowers on her mother's dress.

The baby snoozed peacefully in a cute cotton romper decorated with tiny cars and trains; the matching hat was tucked inside his mother's straw handbag. In addition to the brightly coloured cars and trains, the fabric was also printed with one highly appropriate word: *trésor* or "treasure." What a treasure this little mite was to the two women, young and old, who took turns holding him throughout the Mass!

It was the young mother's turn during the closing prayers. The baby was awake now, chewing contentedly on part of his hand. His mother stood close to his grandmother, both of them sharing one hymn book. The younger woman, already wise in the ways of babies, swayed gently in time to the music. Mother and daughter sang together, along with everyone else in the church, a hymn which expresses our wonder and gratitude for life.

We live in a world that continues to grow and change under God's watchful, loving eye. Anyone who cared to notice could have seen the age-old cycle of birth and renewal played out in the three generations of one family at Mass that day. They stood there singing, savouring every word of the hymn, that much-loved tribute to the Creator of all that is beautiful, alive and inspiring in our world. Yes indeed, Lord, how great Thou art.

All you babies in arms, bless the Lord. All you gently swaying young mothers, bless the Lord. All you proud and smiling grandmothers, bless the Lord. Let all creation sing, "How great Thou art."

Work

Wheelchair Accessible?

I provide bookkeeping and secretarial services to small businesses, and my work takes me somewhere different every day: to doctors' offices, retail stores, private homes. One of my favourite places to work is a bright, cheerful architects' studio on a bustling mid-town street.

Richard, my client, is an architectural consultant in a highly specialized area: a town planner working exclusively in nursing home development and construction. Every day that I spend in his office is an education.

I may be busy with my bookkeeping, but because of the open-plan layout, it is impossible to ignore the other work going on around me. I hear every telephone conversation, see many of the architectural drawings. Once upon a time, I was woefully ignorant of how hospitals or senior citizens' homes are planned or constructed. Now I know.

Someone has to think about the details that most of us ignore. Is the carpet strong enough to withstand constant wear and tear from wheelchairs and walkers? Is the pattern on the wallpaper too confusing for residents with Alzheimer's disease? Is the staff room large enough for the nurses and assistants? One day I overheard a discussion about the quality of food served in one notorious residence. My client indignantly told a colleague, "If those penny-pinching politicians had to eat there for a week, then you'd see how fast the meals would improve!"

I sit at my desk balancing ledgers, making cheques, preparing financial statements, the standard routine of numbers and money, just a few hours every month. Those who work there regularly have devoted a lifetime to a different agenda: the physical needs of the elderly.

So next time you're in a chronic-care hospital, a senior's residence, a nursing home, take a moment to *look*. Someone, a real human being, is responsible for what you see around you. All too often these buildings could be described as "warehouses" because of poor and insensitive planning. On the other hand, if the living space is comfortable and intelligently designed, if every resident has access to a window and all the doorways are wheelchair accessible, say a prayer of thanks. Thank God for people like Richard, those who know that bricks and mortar have an impact on human dignity, who plan and measure and even argue on behalf of those who can no longer care for themselves.

O Lord of architects and designers, if someday I must live in a residence because of sickness or old age, please make it a home built by someone who cared about human dignity.

Laundry

In September 1970, I moved into a modest apartment near the university for my final year of student life, wildly excited about the prospects of having my own place at last. When it was my turn to cook, I impressed my roommates by serving *coq au vin* and *gratin aux fruits de mer*, specialties learned from Julia Child's cookbooks and attempted for the very first time in my new kitchen. Living on my own was certainly a wonderful adventure!

Until I ran out of clean clothes. My childhood training in housework, while fairly comprehensive, had neglected one major appliance: the washing machine. My mother expected us to help around the house in many ways, but she always insisted on doing the laundry herself. As a result, in embarrassed desperation I now had to ask my roommates for advice. At age 21, I could make delicious, flaky pastry but the dials on a washing machine defeated me. I soon learned my way around the washer and dryer, but laundry was never my favourite chore.

Then, years later, on one of my first trips to Italy, I saw something that permanently changed my perspective. One day, while visiting relatives, we saw our cousin standing beside a fountain in the *piazza*. In a scene right out of the Middle Ages, she and a dozen other women, equipped with soap and scrubbing boards, stood washing their families' clothes in the town square. I was horrified. In spite of her comfortable home, our cousin couldn't use her shiny new washing machine because the water pressure in that part of town was too low. So, there she was, a woman exactly my age, laughing and joking as she scrubbed away in the freezing cold water, her hands chapped and rough. If my four grandparents hadn't left Southern Italy for a new life in Canada, that might well have been me! Fiddling with the dials on an automatic washer and dryer suddenly looked more inviting.

A year later, I came across some photographs of the famous 19th-century mystic Thérèse of Lisieux. One particular image of this beloved saint caught my attention. In fact, it comes to mind whenever I set out to tackle the piles of sheets and towels waiting to be washed, because it makes me even more grateful for my modern appliances. The photographer captured the Little Flower and her fellow nuns in their black and white Carmelite habits, all on their knees looking quietly virtuous. These good women are not praying. They are kneeling around a vast tub full of hot, soapy water, doing the convent's laundry.

O Lord of servants and housekeepers, thank you for showing me that even saints have to do housework.

Helping Hands

The day started badly. I arrived at the glamorous store in the downtown fashion district for my regular day of bookkeeping just as the building opened in the morning. I walked in and my heart sank. In spite of the brilliant sunshine outside, it was positively freezing indoors. Someone had left the air conditioning on all night again!

Glad that I was wearing heavy jeans, a long-sleeved shirt *and* a warm jacket, I proceeded to the office at the back. Here, if possible, it was even colder. Furthermore, in the week since my last visit, a cyclone of disorganization seemed to have struck the room. Half-finished payroll material cluttered the top of the overloaded desk; a sea of faxes lay curled up on the rug by the chair; boxes of stationery leaned precariously against the back wall. To get to the desk, I had to navigate through an obstacle course of catalogues piled in the middle of the floor. I surveyed the chaos, lamenting to myself: "And I have to work here all day!"

When calm reason returned, I moved the payroll material off the desk and began to sort the files. My hands were soon dry and dusty, and turning blue in the frigid temperature. By zipping up my jacket, gritting my teeth, and taking regular breaks every half hour, I coped with the cold, hoping that the temperature would eventually return to normal. I played clever games with myself: "You can take a break as soon as the next bank statement balances." At lunch I thumbed through a gardening magazine in the variety store across the road; the flame-coloured bloom on the cover reminded me of "Desert Peace," the latest addition to our rose garden at home. The very idea of roses and deserts warmed me. Somehow the time passed and the work got done.

As the afternoon wore on I played one final game with myself: "Just finish this page, then you can buy a treat on your next break." At three o'clock, I trekked down the street to a warm, clean, perfectly organized cosmetics store. Here was a place of refuge for a few minutes at least! I purchased a jar of cream called "Helping Hands."

Later on, home at last, I tried out the cream. It was an instant success. The calming scent of chamomile and lavender was exactly what my sensitive hands needed after a day handling reams of dry paper, in offices neat or messy.

I reflected on this paradox: because I was working in a chaotic, uncomfortable place, I took that late afternoon break. Only then could unseen "helping hands" lead me down the street to the store, and a soothing, useful product to enjoy in the days to come.

O Lord the Carpenter, you too once worked with your hands. Help us create offices and factories that are gentle to our bodies and kind to our souls.

The Taj Mahal of Showers

At last the renovations were over! The chaos of noise and dust subsided, the plumber packed up his tools, and the contractor submitted one final bill. There in the basement, in a cubbyhole once part of the laundry area, now stood a splendid bathroom. Or, more accurately, a shower room. A wise-cracking cousin, the family comedian, surveyed the expanse of gleaming white tiles, turned to Steve, the hero of this story, and quipped, "Looks like the Taj Mahal to me." The nickname stuck.

The Taj Mahal of showers had been designed with a specific purpose in mind, for in those days, Steve had an excellent job as an engineer. After a hard day on a muddy job site he would leave his safety boots at the side door and proceed directly downstairs to wash up before dinner. He loved the rush of cool water on his hot, dusty skin and afterwards joked how he felt "ten pounds lighter" now that he was clean.

Then, one summer, engineering jobs went the way of the dodo bird. For the next few months Steve kept to himself, took long walks, lost weight from stress. Jobs didn't return the next spring either. To earn his keep, as he called it, he gradually took over more and more of the housework, the grocery shopping, the laundry, the cooking. The shower in the basement was still his private oasis, but there were no muddy boots at the side door.

Time passed. When the job market picked up, Steve was pushing 60. The comedian-cousin might call him "a tough old goat," but to those doing the hiring, he was merely old.

The Taj Mahal of showers, however, was still busy, for now our hero worked up a healthy sweat at home. In the summer he gardened, zealously defending his vegetables from the local squirrels. In winter he waged war on any snow that dared to fall on his pristine driveway. He turned out to be an inspired cook, and took great pride in having a special meal ready and waiting when the others returned home in the evening. Finally the family comedian announced that our hero was no longer "unemployed": he was now so old he was actually "retired."

Everyone still called the shower in the basement "The Taj Mahal." A more fitting name might have been "The Baptismal Font." After living with one less paycheque for so long, Steve's family was less concerned about the almighty dollar, more interested in simple pleasures; they had become kinder and more patient. Everyone had been transformed, as if by water and the Holy Spirit, and each was richer for the experience.

O Lord of the empty spaces, those of us learning to cope with Less are sometimes forgotten in a world obsessed with having More. But you remember us.

Home Sweet Home

It was an ordinary day in an office for me, shuffling papers, pushing pencils, crunching numbers. First order of business: the documents for the sale of townhouses in a suburban development. I planned to record the various details of the purchases – lot numbers, sale prices, owners' names, closing dates – so sitting down at a desk I started to work.

After a while, routine set in and I began to wonder about the real people behind the names and the numbers: the Sharons and Ians, Brendas, Xaviers and Veronicas who bought the townhouses my client was building. He had told me a little about the project – the modestly priced houses offering good value for young people just starting out. The initial deposit, a mere $500, made home ownership a real possibility for them. My client was proud of the project, not just as an investment opportunity, but as a valuable contribution to the stock of affordable housing in his community.

As I continued my work, I thought about my younger days, when I was very much like the Sharons and Ians: just starting out. When I moved into my first house, the living room furniture consisted of family hand-me-downs, a few carefully planned purchases and a couple of lawn chairs. There was one beat-up floor lamp, a relic from my parents' basement, strategically placed between the living and dining rooms until I could afford *two* light fixtures. I remember stripping old wood and refinishing the mantelpiece; reclaiming the overgrown garden in need of loving care after years of neglect; painting bookshelves, choosing wallpaper, eventually having enough money for rugs. How rewarding, exciting and challenging it was setting up my first house! How comforting to realize that young people have the same dreams and goals today, hoping, saving, scheming, planning for the future in their first homes.

Eventually I finished my work on the documents and I was free to move on to another project. But my imagination remained behind in the townhouse development. Why are homes so important to us? Far beyond our need for shelter, even a humble home represents the fundamental human yearning for security, comfort, aesthetic expression, cultural identity.

Jesus himself recognized our age-old human desire for *home* when he reassured his anxious disciples about their place in his future (John 14:2). Using the image of a large mansion, Jesus promised to prepare a special place for his followers when he returned to his Father's kingdom. These words still resonate in my heart today as I remember the promise: in our Heavenly Father's house there are many rooms, a place where everyone will feel welcome, comfortable, secure and ultimately at home.

O Lord, you were born in a stable. Even as I dream of the perfect home on earth, I yearn for the palaces of your Father's kingdom in heaven.

Family Business

I stood at the automated bank machine clutching a fistful of papers. A multitude of transactions – deposits, withdrawals, transfers – demanded a certain concentration. But eventually I noticed a young woman and her small daughter at the machine next to mine. The little girl wanted to "help" with the family banking: pushing buttons, sealing envelopes. Of course, her help made their transactions take twice as long as usual, so the young woman meekly apologized to the others waiting patiently in line. One good-natured fellow quipped, "Mother's Little Helper," and everyone smiled.

My banking marathon was soon finished, but those three innocent little words stuck in my memory for hours. I too started my long career in office administration and accounting in just that way: helping Mom and Dad when I was little. During the Christmas holidays, we happily tagged along to "Mom's Office" to help with the annual mailing of calendars to customers. Likewise, nearly every Sunday we drove to "Dad's Store" to help my father check the boiler, make sure none of the pipes had frozen in winter, and generally keep an eye on things. Those regular visits to Dad's Store and Mom's Office taught me valuable lessons about the non-stop responsibilities of a family business.

Later, as young teenagers, my sisters and I worked every year for three wonderful weeks in our booth at the Canadian National Exhibition, the ultimate summer job at the time. Poppy, our grandfather, chauffeured us to the bus stop very early in the mornings on *his* way to work. When we were older, Mom found a variety of equally educational jobs for us back in the office. I remember a maxim often repeated by Uncle Ted whenever he lectured us about keeping order: when work seemed overwhelming, he said, "Start with the first piece of paper on the top of the pile." I learned a lot by working in a family business.

Jesus the Teenager touches a place deep in my heart. He blithely reassures Mary and Joseph after they'd spent three days frantically searching for him. He has not been "lost" at all, he explains, cool as a cucumber. He has been in the Temple, checking out the action at the scene of his Father's business (Luke 2:41-51).

St. Luke has traditionally been regarded as a physician, a career often passed down in families. Is that why he is the only one of the evangelists to include this insightful scene in his Gospel? Perhaps he had first-hand experience of children following in their parents' footsteps. Like the woman letting her small daughter "help" at the bank machine, St. Luke seems to have known that children need and want to learn about work at an early age, whether the work is "saving the world" or merely doing its banking.

O Lord whom we call the Carpenter, teach us to appreciate the value and meaning of work. Help us find work that uses our talents and natural abilities.

Am I Working or Playing?

Alison's music studio can be found on the third floor of an attractive renovated building in the heart of the inner city. What was once an old factory has been converted into offices for advertising agencies and small law firms, musicians and artisans, tenants who appreciate a downtown location and spacious floor plans. Everywhere the interior walls, brick not plaster, remind visitors of the industrial heritage of this site. The high ceilings and tall windows, enormous exposed pipes and metal fire escapes are relics from a different age.

Take away the long halls separating the offices, and it's easy to imagine bygone days when a different sort of work took place within these walls. Once upon a time buildings like this were used for light manufacturing; there were small assembly lines, huge rooms full of machinery and equipment, bales of cotton and wool piled high to the ceiling. Today fax machines and computers occupy offices built on a different scale. But "work" is "work," then and now, and in her studio Alison works.

The people who come here when she is working, however, are here to "play." For Alison, a highly accomplished performer and recording artist, also teaches music. On one recent Saturday morning, 13 adults attended her workshop on Renaissance Music in Germany. Alison's students work at conventional jobs during the week: a lawyer, an architect, a doctor, the owner of a small business, a couple of teachers, an artist. But Saturday was time for play.

Playing music, of course, but more broadly, making time for the rest and recreation that belong to life away from work. Nevertheless, those who came to play were given challenging work to do: difficult pieces with tricky counting and unfamiliar sharps and flats, and in one case, a peculiar clef to decipher. After a while, the group at play needed a refreshment break, because they had worked hard all morning.

The line between "work" and "play" is nicely blurred in a place like Alison's studio. As a professional she has experienced her own share of labour, preparing for a concert or recording session. She likewise expects her students to put forth a concerted effort: to learn, to improve, to keep up with the group. The students return, week after week, because learning is fun, music provides its own reward, and because using our human talents and creativity is a source of joy — even when we have to work in order to play.

O Lord of students and teachers, I am grateful for activities that challenge my mind while refreshing my spirit.

Play

Postcards from Heaven

I am a morning person. No matter how early it is, I can bounce out of bed with a song on my lips and a prayer in my heart. By late afternoon, however, my body rhythms are reversed; then I'm often tired, hungry, even cranky. At just such a low ebb I arrived home one day last week, feeling more than a little weary. Waiting inside, along with the bills in the mail, was a postcard that revived my drooping spirits but gave me much to ponder for the rest of the evening.

The postcard was a typical photograph of Nature at her grandest: an Oregon coastline shrouded in fog and mist with hundreds of gulls soaring over sand and sea. Marda, our correspondent, appreciated our love of such special places; in fact, our friendship dated back to 1977 and the very beginning of a bird-watching expedition to Baja California, Mexico. Thanks to Marda's expert advice about travel south of the border, we experienced the unspoiled coastal wilderness at its best.

If there is one memory guaranteed to cheer me up during the low point of my day, it is the recollection of those carefree weeks camping on the beach in the Baja. Dolphins splashing happily around the offshore islands early in the morning; seals sunbathing on the rocks at noon; osprey fishing on the beach for their supper: we were privileged to share our ocean playground with a host of wild creatures all day long. Marda's postcard brought back a flood of happy memories: memories of the grandeur, but also the playfulness, to be found everywhere in God's Creation.

The strange thing is, when we received her postcard Marda had already been dead for eight years. After the first shock of seeing her distinctive handwriting, I was more than a little puzzled. Who sent this postcard? Was it some kind of morbid joke? Then I noticed the postmark: *June 3, 1983!*

On an afternoon when Life seemed bleak and cheerless, Marda's postcard appeared, seemingly from beyond the grave. "How had it finally been delivered?" I wondered. "Why did it come today of all days? Did it arrive to remind me of the enduring bonds of friendship; to revive memories of holidays in the past; to inspire plans for more such happy days here in the present?"

I like to reply promptly to my mail, so here goes:

"Dear Marda,

Thanks so much for your postcard from Heaven. It arrived just the other day! The picture reminds me that, somewhere in the world, the sun is shining and birds soar over the ocean. Rest in peace.

Love,
Bertha"

O Lord of friendship, help me to share myself with others as you have shared yourself with me.

Making Roses

"Nicole" doesn't really like it here in Canada. Her first summer passed uneventfully but, like many newcomers, she received a terrible shock when winter touched her with its icy hand. Her friends did everything to help her cope with the cold, but during this, her second summer, she is not as healthy as last year. I am afraid that we may lose her, in spite of all our careful attention. "Nicole" is a rose from South America.

We first met "Nicole" in a flower shop specializing in exotic imports from South American growers. She is a splendid beauty with deep red on one side of her petals and dusty silver on the reverse. The owner scoffed when we suggested trying to propagate "Nicole" at home. Scepticism only sweetened the challenge. It took a few attempts but we finally succeeded, thanks to a combination of patience, rooting hormone and a homemade greenhouse (coat hangers and clear plastic garbage bags work just fine). Last year we planted "Nicole" in our garden and she bloomed twice for us. This year? We're still hoping.

If "Nicole" is eventually unable to cope with the rigours of life in Canada, we will miss her but there are other roses better suited to this northern climate. We have many two-tone beauties to enjoy, roses like "Double Delight" and "Flaming Peace." I love the names of the new varieties, names like "Sheer Bliss" and "Fragrant Cloud," suggesting the heaven-on-earth loveliness associated with this fabled and ancient flower.

Right now by our dining room window, yet another homemade greenhouse takes up a lot of floor space. Every few days we peer into its murky depths, for almost hidden in the gloom is another cutting. If this nameless beauty succeeds in putting down roots, we will eventually have a splendid yellow-and-orange companion to put beside "Nicole" in the garden.

Although we can buy roses easily enough, there is something especially satisfying about "making" them ourselves. I say "making" with reservations. If ever there is a time to feel humble in the presence of our Maker – the Creator ultimately responsible for the glories of the whole universe – it is while trying to propagate roses at home. Just as children marvel at a tray of tiny seeds germinating in a classroom window, so I look at the few roses we have "made" and stand in awe. Some scientists see the hand of God within the marvels of the solar system, as they watch the planets calmly travel in their orbits millions of miles away. I see the same Hand in the garden outside my front door.

O Lord of astronomers and gardeners, I am grateful to be part of your creation of sun, moon, stars – and roses.

Raindrops

The car was packed and ready to go. Packed? Loaded down, every spare inch of space stuffed full of equipment! For this camping trip we needed more gear than usual, especially in the dining department. Karen and her little boy, Robert, were joining us for the weekend and I had volunteered to organize the meals. I bought apple juice and extra milk, and found more camping plates in the basement. Finally we were off. Now all we needed was good weather.

In the week before we left, the weather had been not merely good but perfect, so as luck would have it, the sky clouded over as soon as we arrived at the park and started to put up our tents. Dismayed by the threat of rain, we worked quickly, but soon it was coming down in earnest. My worst fear was coming true! What would we do with Robert if it rained? Reflecting on the perversity of the Canadian summer (sunny weekdays followed by wet weekends), I muttered to myself, "Why now, Lord?" We took shelter in our tents and prepared to wait.

Robert reacted to the sudden shower in a different way. The drumming of the rain on the tent was a new and frightening sound for someone who was just 18 months old. He started to cry. A new toy, a colourful reversible car complete with reversible driver, was the perfect distraction. Robert stopped crying, the shower was soon over, and it was safe to move back outside. The three adults dried off the lawn chairs; predictably, the child headed straight for the puddles and the mud.

Notice the contrast between our reactions to raindrops on the camping trip. Bertha the Adult hates to have her carefully arranged plans altered. Robert the Child, on the other hand, is happily oblivious to the concept of careful planning. And while he may be frightened by the unfamiliar sound of the raindrops, he enjoys the puddles and mud that the rain leaves behind.

Perhaps the best way to experience the great Camping Trip of Life is to be a combination of both adult and child. Mature enough to pack the apple juice and milk, to remember the extra plates, to appreciate the soothing sound of raindrops on the tent. But still enough of a child to splash a little in the puddles and to take life as it comes, moment by moment, rain or shine.

O Lord of sunshine and raindrops, teach me to treasure the messy, chaotic, unstructured side of my life.

French Perfume

It was our last morning in Paris. Joan and I were on a three-month trip to Europe, the experience of a lifetime! The year was 1970 and as typical starving students, we had a limited budget. Thanks to inexpensive cafés and a succession of cheap little hotels, we stretched our money as far as possible. Paris, however, was a week-long assault on our careful fiscal planning. Even the most affordable restaurant charged an outrageous fortune, so we resorted to buying food in grocery stores and having picnics in the parks. Granted, it is not exactly a hardship to enjoy *pâté en croute* in the Luxembourg Gardens, but pâtés and gardens notwithstanding, we had to watch our pennies, or rather our *francs*.

So, on our last morning in Paris, Joan and I carefully looked over the French money we had left. Neither of us had much, but for those travelling on less than $10 per day, every *centime* counts. Because of fluctuating exchange rates, we always tried to spend every last *peseta* or *guilder* or *drachma* before moving on to another country and another currency. In Paris, we counted and thought and counted up again. Perhaps we had just enough left for two bottles of French perfume.

We quickly found a perfume store and looked at every single bottle on the shelves. What was the best way to spend every last *franc* and each have a bottle of French perfume, the ultimate souvenir of Paris? I wanted one of the light, fresh scents popular with girls back then. I can't remember the name but it had a striped green label and it was cheap. Alas,

Joan's favourite cost somewhat more. We had a problem. No matter how we pooled our money, or what we chose to buy, we didn't seem to have enough for each of us to carry away a precious bottle when we said *au revoir* to Paris.

Meanwhile the sales clerk, a typically glamorous Parisienne, had been listening to our discussions. Finally she had heard enough. She boldly asked, *en français* of course, "What is the problem?" Less boldly I replied, "Two bottles, not enough money." She looked over our choices, counted our precious *francs*, and said, "*Ça suffit* – that is enough." Then she wrapped up our choices. Perhaps she cared more about our appreciation of Parisian traditions than our strict ability to pay for them.

I have wonderful memories of Paris: my first glimpse of the "Winged Victory" in the Louvre, the Organ Mass at Notre Dame cathedral, the famous gardens where we dined in grand if economical splendour. But I have a particularly warm memory of that glamorous shopkeeper. *Merci beaucoup, Mademoiselle Inconnue.* On behalf of student travellers everywhere, many thanks, not for the perfume, long gone, names forgotten, but for your gesture of spontaneous generosity.

O Lord of frankincense and myrrh, every precious perfume and fragrant flower is your gift to me. Let my senses rejoice!

Backwards Day

My father was a man of many moods, some of them very bleak indeed. Thankfully for the family business, he was always at his most gracious between nine and five, but there was a darker side to his charm: a theatrical capacity for melodramatic anger. On the other hand, Dad was equally enthusiastic about high-spirited games, at his best a shining example of playfulness and fun.

A gifted raconteur with a stock of hilarious stories (including an account of sneaking into Maple Leaf Gardens as a kid to see the first hockey game played there), Dad held court at his store, surrounded by customers and friends – judges and celebrities, errand boys and famous chefs. He knew the words to innumerable old songs, and could often be heard crooning such forgotten gems as "Must be jelly 'cause jam don't shake like that." Like bit players in countless old movies, his friends had names like "Lucky" and "Pete the Greek," characters straight out of a Damon Runyan story. Dad knew something about life with a capital "L."

Yet Dad was also intensely religious, often going to church every day in Lent. He was never without a rosary in his pocket, and insisted that his daughters "attend Catholic schools even if they have to be bussed there, end of discussion." He detested fish, yet in our pre-Vatican II household, meat was forbidden on Fridays. He suffered, not necessarily in silence, but he ate the fish my mother served.

Dad's uncertain temper was usually soothed by a nice meal (except perhaps on Fridays). Since my mother was an excellent cook, he was often in a good mood during the family dinner hour. On one memorable occasion he inaugurated the first official "Backwards Day." Dad sat down for dinner with his suit jacket on backwards and rearranged the table. Then, to conclude his performance of eating "backwards," he balanced the salad bowl on his head. Everyone went wild with excitement, and when some of the salad spilled, as expected, there were more explosions of laughter. Many years later the memory is still as fresh as the lyrics to Dad's favourite songs.

He died one April Fool's Day. Friends who heard the sad news said, "Tell me you're just joking." The funeral home was crowded with family, friends and old cronies, even the men in tears. The cortège to the church was blocks long, traffic snarled in all directions. After the funeral, and in spite of a foot of wet spring snow, everyone trooped along for the burial at Mount Hope Cemetery. This was followed by a huge party at home, the perfect send-off. Dad would have loved every minute.

O Lord who spoke so lovingly of your heavenly Father, help us to understand and love the fathers who shape our lives.

Deck the Halls

Christmas Eve, morning. I rolled out of bed smugly content with my holiday preparations. The tree had been up since early December; the gifts bought, wrapped, delivered. I had steamed the fig pudding weeks ago; the cranberry compote nestled in the back of the refrigerator. Now for a leisurely brunch with Joan, my oldest friend – a visit that would turn into an unexpected learning experience.

As soon as I walked into her house, I noticed the white pine boughs decorating Joan's mantel. My friend has always been artistic and clever with her hands, and looking at her beautiful arrangement in green, white and gold, my heart was stabbed with pangs of wistful longing. I hid my feelings with a joke and a compliment: "I'm envious of your gorgeous decorations!" Joan's reply only intensified my longings, for she said, "You could do this, too." Then, being practical (and thrifty as well), she told me just what to buy at the garden centre near my house; everything was on sale because it was already Christmas Eve.

Christmas Eve, afternoon. I walked back into my house holding a huge bag of half-price evergreens, miniature lights and red velvet bows, sweating from fear. I was about to make something with my hands! The prospect of feeding 20 relatives on Christmas Day was laughably easy, cooking being second nature to me. But home decorating, like sewing or crafts of any kind, is foreign territory. I am woefully inept with any project requiring manual dexterity. Many years ago Sister Mary Alban wrote on my report card, "Bertha cannot cut straight or colour within the lines." But today, Christmas Eve, I kept reminding myself of Joan's words: "You could do this, too."

I had to make another trip to the garden centre, having seriously underestimated the amount of greenery required. I pinched my fingers a few times on the stems of the holly and had to rearrange the lights more than once before they looked just right. But when I had finished, there it was: one decorated banister in my dining room! Full of simple pride, I took a couple of photos to remind me how to do this again next year.

Christmas Eve, midnight Mass. Our church was beautifully decorated, as always. I thought of my own handiwork at home – one decorated banister – finished just in time for Christmas Day, and offered a prayer. O little child of Bethlehem, thanks for making this the first (I hope) of many Christmas seasons where I try to deck the halls (or at least the banister in the dining room) all by myself!

O Lord of pine cones and fir trees, thank you for friends who help me to celebrate your birthday in the most perfectly childlike way: playing with coloured lights and pretty velvet bows.

Small World

A Food Court in a Mall. Someone has moved the tables and set up a wide-screen TV. It's late in the day so almost everyone who stops to watch the World Cup of Soccer stays for only a brief moment. Except for one well-dressed woman, the quintessential successful executive. She sees that Germany is playing and instantly sits down. Here is a real fan. In heavily accented English she cheers the players on, even calling them by name. Others stare at her in astonishment. She knows more about the game than anyone else present!

A Café at Lunchtime. The tables are more crowded than usual, the staff even less attentive. Very few people are eating the veal sandwiches, grilled *panini*, slices of pizza. The tiny cups of espresso and tall glasses of cappuccino are likewise ignored. Food and drink are secondary to the action, everyone's attention focused closely, but not quietly, on the small television screen mounted above the door. Everyone is rooting for the Italians, including any Blacks and Asians present; indeed some of the most vociferous Italian supporters are doing their cheering in Spanish. When the game ends with a loss for Italy, the crowd moans, curses and finally melts away, back to work.

A Downtown Gym. Most of the television sets near the bikes and treadmills are tuned to the soccer game. The sound is turned off, but so what? We start with the national anthems. The camera pans over the two silently singing teams. First the favourites, mostly small and dark, whose racial mix includes aboriginal peoples, African slaves and waves of

Mediterranean immigrants. Then their opponents, shaggy blond giants, obviously the descendants of Vikings.

Even if the sound were turned on, few in the gym would understand the words the players are singing. But words notwithstanding, we know full well the meaning of their songs. These national anthems have little to do with political boundaries drawn on maps made long ago. The players are singing about their joy in playing on a world stage, sending a greeting to the friends and relatives watching in Brazil or Denmark, shouting their support and encouragement to the others on their team. Ultimately, they are expressing their love for the place they call home.

A Cozy Restaurant. The owners may come from southern Italy but their restaurant has become the centre of a huge victory party *à la française.* Two of the city's most distinguished French chefs are there waving flags, singing songs, proposing toasts with champagne. The Italian, South American and Middle Eastern waiters graciously accept the good-natured French teasing. This is Toronto, one of the most ethnically diverse cities in the world. This is Canada, multicultural home to immigrants from a hundred countries. This is the Global Village. A game played in one country has been watched, analyzed, lamented, celebrated by *billions* of people everywhere. No matter who wins or loses, all of us are winners when we appreciate the diversity of this one small world.

O Lord of black and white, yellow and red, my heart is touched by any celebration that involves the whole human family — the more the merrier!

Simple Comforts

A Bath

A Tote Bag

A Sandwich

A Comforter

The Radio

A Coat

New Shoes

A Bath

Have you ever thought about the simple act of taking a bath?

You, the bather-to-be, enter a quiet and private space, one of the few places where you can still find solitude and silence. You turn a tap and voilà, hot water appears, like magic. Perhaps you add some Epsom salts or fragrant oils to the maelstrom of gushing waters, to soothe or soften your skin. A comforting steamy atmosphere starts to build in the room. Your bath is nearly ready.

As you undress, you gently but firmly leave behind everything that belongs to the outside world: the world of work or sleep or exercise. Taking a moment to anticipate your future needs, you place a clean towel near the edge of the bath or hang a bathrobe nearby.

Stepping into the bath, you imagine yourself stepping outside your regular life, stepping away from the cares of work, stepping up to the part of yourself that already knows how to relax. Once in the tub, you stretch out.

Perhaps your bath includes a plastic pillow to cushion your head, or an old towel coiled into a makeshift headrest. You make yourself comfortable. Perhaps you wash or play with the toys the children left behind. Whatever you do is up to you: there is no right or wrong way to bathe. No one is there to watch and comment.

If time permits, you plan to get your full money's worth from the hot water, daydreaming in the warm, lazy atmosphere for 15, 20 or even 30 minutes. If the ledge of the bath is wide enough, you bring along a cup of tea in winter or a glass of something long and cold in summer. You may even enjoy a book or magazine as you soak. Meanwhile, your muscles have started to relax, the tension in your mind and spirit floating away in the water. And you recognize this ordinary act of daily hygiene, taking a bath, as an opportunity to experience simple pleasure.

Now might be a good time to sigh a simple prayer of gratitude: for clean water, fresh towels, gentle soap. To remember those who live in societies where indoor plumbing is an unimaginable luxury. To spend a few moments in thanksgiving for the possessions which have enhanced your bath: the plants on the windowsill, the soft bathrobe, the scented oils. To give thanks for your time, your body, your ability to enjoy this bath: the many blessings you regularly take for granted. To resolve, once this bath is over, to be more grateful for the gift of simple pleasure.

O Lord of still and silent waters, forgive me for the times when I have taken the simple pleasures of life for granted.

A Tote Bag

On a dismal day last winter, I went to buy face cream and found that my favourite brand came with a "free gift." This was a heavy plastic tote bag in a gorgeous spring-time shade of pink. It proved to be just what I needed: waterproof, with comfortable handles; the right size to hold my lunch, some office supplies, and a magazine to read on the subway. And it really was a very pretty shade of pink.

A week or so later, I tried out the new tote. Walking along the sidewalk, I took a moment to appreciate the deep blue sky of a bright, sunny afternoon. Then, turning the corner, with the setting sun behind me, I saw my shadow. And what I saw made my heart leap with joy and amazement. The sunlight streamed right through my clear plastic tote bag: the shadow on the sidewalk was *bright pink*. I was carrying part of a rainbow in my hand. Thanks to my new tote bag I had become a walking stained-glass window!

Now, whenever the sun is bright and strong behind me, I take a moment to notice the pink shadow cast by my tote bag. In some ways the bag and its contents are a symbol of work: my obligation to be productive, to satisfy my clients, to earn money to support myself. In all honesty, work can be an irksome burden, much heavier than a mere tote bag, especially when I am tired or discouraged. The very need to carry a tote bag is itself a sign of a responsible, organized, even frugal, lifestyle: there inside is the simple lunch made at home, and something to read on the way to and from work.

But thanks to my transparent tote bag, no matter where I go — to a pleasant office or to a stressful one — I carry a bright pink light beside me.

Noticing the pink shadow on the sidewalk, I also laugh a little inside. For my tote bag is fast becoming a symbol of Grace itself. I carry an unexpected Light in my life, something which costs me nothing and never fails to cheer me as I walk through my day. Something practical, beautiful and joyful in my life. My tote bag reminds me to offer up a silent prayer of thanksgiving for the unexpected "gifts" which touch my heart.

O Lord of the rainbow, you give me eyes to see and strength to carry my burdens. Thank you for lighting the way for me.

A Sandwich

written very early in the morning

This morning I will make a sandwich for my lunch. In fact, I'm planning to make my very favourite kind, following a recipe given to me 30 years ago by an old friend. Harriet told me to mix "one tin of tuna, two hard-boiled eggs, lots of chopped celery and a little mayonnaise." She had created this unique combination when her children were small and money was tight. As I assemble the ingredients I will think, "I'll be having a treat for lunch today."

When I unwrap my sandwich at lunch time, I'll remember Harriet and the other cooking secrets she shared with me, such as "how to make really nice pastry." I'll remember her short grey hair, very much the same colour as mine is today, her astounding facility with crossword puzzles, her long drives alone in the countryside. Funny how a simple sandwich for lunch can evoke so many happy memories.

At noon I'll eat my sandwich in whatever downtown office is my workplace for the day. I've been taking a brown bag lunch for over 35 years, so my meal may very well remind me of my old high school, The Abbey, and the lunches my mother packed for us year after year. She made thousands of sandwiches in those days – for herself, for the kids, sometimes even for Dad! There was always a treat tucked away in our brown paper bags: a few cookies or a slice of cake. But oh, those sandwiches: tuna, egg, ham, salmon salad, cheese, peanut butter, sliced chicken. Funny how eating lunch at work can remind me so much of my mother and all she did for her children when we were at school.

After lunch, I'll step outside for a breath of fresh air. Rain or shine, there will be people begging on the street. Yesterday, I saw a mother and three bedraggled children sitting right on the cold, dirty sidewalk; I gave them the cookies left over from my lunch. If I feel noble and virtuous for eating a homemade sandwich at my desk – compared to those who have wolfed down a T-bone steak and a double martini in a fancy restaurant – I have only to look at those poor souls on the street corners to appreciate my good fortune.

That good fortune has less to do with my bank balance and more to do with my memory bank. It contains so many images: creative friends who shared their recipes with me; my loving family; years of gainful employment and all the sandwiches I've carried to work. I may not remember the customary words to "Grace after Meals," but here's my own version: God, help me to be grateful for a simple sandwich prepared with loving memories in my own kitchen.

O Lord who blessed the loaves and fishes, day after day my simple sandwich gives me many reasons to be grateful.

A Comforter

One June a few years ago I spent some time at a nearby retreat centre. My bare, cheerless room, painted institutional beige, had a nondescript carpet on the floor. An ancient armchair lurked in a dingy corner, a lumpy bed sagged against one wall, a well-worn desk leaned against another. Whatever prayers or meditations might take place here, those on retreat would never be distracted by the luxurious furnishings!

Nevertheless, during my nights in these dismal surroundings, I definitely noticed the room's one attractive feature: the comforter that lay on the bed. All my life I have slept under thick woollen blankets and old-fashioned quilts. This was my very first experience with a new-fangled duvet, and it was a revelation. What a wonderful innovation – light, warm, cosy!

Soon after the retreat, an advertisement for Canadian-made duvets caught my eye. The "off-season sale" was near one of my regular clients, so one Friday afternoon after work, I bought one of these miracles of modern bedding.

My new comforter – little more than a puffy filling, an oversized cotton cover and lots of air – is light, warm and cosy. Making the bed has never been easier. If I'm feeling happy, its presence enhances the glow of well-being that surrounds me; if I'm feeling sad, it comforts me, just as the name says. Reading in bed has never been nicer. I stored our old woollen blanket in a moth-proof bag and prepared to enjoy the new duvet all year 'round.

Then one day last winter, I presented a guided meditation based on Psalm 23: "The Lord is my shepherd." At the line about "resting in fresh green pastures," I described the hot, arid climate of ancient Israel; in a dry southern landscape, lying down in a cool green meadow is a most attractive prospect. Since this picture is hardly inviting during a rigorous northern winter, I suggested instead that we let our imagination take us to a beautiful bedroom in a comfortable country inn. I asked my audience to imagine the pastel walls, the soft carpet underfoot, and finally, the fluffy comforter on the bed.

I suggested that, for the moment, we replace the Shepherd with an attentive Innkeeper, someone keenly aware of each guest's need for rest, peace and comfort: a gracious Host sensitive to all human yearnings. I reminded everyone that the theme of this psalm, with its focus on everyday pleasures, is the portrait of One who cares about every aspect of human life. Then, thinking about the duvet waiting for me on my own bed, I smiled.

O Lord of innkeepers and shepherds, during the darkest nights and in the bleakest weather, you bring me rest and comfort.

The Radio

I first fell in love with the radio when I was very young. Mom regularly listened to Jack Kent Cooke's "Make-Believe Ballroom" while making dinner and waiting for Dad to come home from work. As she prepared her famous breaded veal cutlets or luscious pot roast, she introduced me to the Big Band hits of Glenn Miller and Tommy Dorsey. On Saturdays she tuned into the Metropolitan Opera broadcasts while putting on the weekly pot of chicken soup. To this day I invariably associate chicken soup with Carmen or Tosca. Now I too listen to the radio while cooking dinner. The music changes but the song remains the same.

Lately, I have noticed that the radio emphasizes yet another unexpected bond in my life: the connection between me in my kitchen here and now, and other people from long ago and/or far away. Thanks to the radio, on any given day I might hear a gospel choir from the South African townships, a string quartet from Prague, a group of yodellers from Switzerland, a percussion ensemble from Japan. Music written by Hildegarde of Bingen, a mediaeval German abbess, is followed by a folk song popular in the American Civil War. From Beethoven to the Beatles, from Gregorian chant to George Gershwin, the radio brings it all into my home absolutely free.

Another special radio memory concerns Christmas. But first, some background about me. I am an early bird – a lark, not an owl – so staying up into the wee hours is never my idea of fun. Yet a few years ago, I was deeply honoured when

I was invited to be lector for midnight Mass. At the very last minute, someone asked me to fill in for an absent eucharistic minister as well. So in addition to reading the scriptures I also gave out communion to hundreds of my fellow Christians. It was a privilege to share the Christmas liturgy with so many people – even if it was well past my bedtime.

Driving home afterwards, already excited from the events of the midnight Mass, and giddy from lack of sleep, I felt like a six-year-old waiting for Santa Claus. Then I discovered that my favourite radio station was broadcasting Christmas music all night long! So, with sleep patterns already disturbed, I listened to my bedside radio far into the night. I rejoiced to hear standard carols as well as highlights from Handel's *Messiah*, a dance from *The Nutcracker,* a movement of Bach's *Christmas Oratorio.*

Looking back on that musical night, I treasure my memory of midnight Mass, a celebration that united me with hundreds of other Christmas worshippers. In the same way, I treasure the magic of radio, which linked me to countless others around the world and down through the ages of time.

O Lord of the airwaves, the good news of your birth – tidings of comfort and joy – fills this world with music, night and day.

A Coat

I first saw the coat on my way to work early one January morning. It was barely visible through the plate-glass windows in a shopping concourse not yet open for the day. All morning at my desk, instead of giving my full attention to the ledgers in front of me, I dreamt about the coat, planning to investigate more fully at lunchtime.

The coat was perfect. A dark green beauty in just the right size, it was long enough to keep me warm on the coldest days, with special features including a cosy hood and sensible storm cuffs in the generous, roomy sleeves. It was made from water-resistant fabric and on sale at a reasonable price. What more could anyone ask? For the rest of the winter I enjoyed my new coat, appreciated the compliments friends paid me, noticed the way it lived up to its billing as "beautiful and practical, designed for years of carefree enjoyment." But most of all I loved the freedom that it represented.

For instance, it gave me freedom to enjoy winter. Covered from head to toe in a warm, water-resistant fabric, I could laugh at any weather forecast. Snuggled into the warmth of my coat, I was free to appreciate the early morning light on the snow, the stark silhouettes of dark trees against pale sky, the hoarfrost on the bushes in my front garden, my very own winter fairyland. Instead of shivering on cold, damp days, I enjoyed being outside, especially on my walks to and from work.

Indeed, my coat symbolized the very freedom to work. Remember the shopping concourse where I found my coat?

Imagine all the other women who buy the coats and suits sold there, the women who work in the nearby office blocks and bank towers. Think about these customers: educated, talented women free to find employment outside the home, to grow and change through the stimulation of a challenging career.

Now, spare a moment to grieve with me for those women forbidden to use their talents by repressive regimes that treat them with contempt, often in the name of custom or religious tradition. These women can't even dream of basic human rights I take for granted: the freedom to study in the field of their choice and to work without harassment; to use their talents in jobs traditional or unconventional; to walk in public along any road, winter or summer.

As I prepare to go outside into the cold of a winter morning, I think gratefully of the freedoms symbolized by my new winter coat.

O Lord of hope and freedom, your message of liberation belongs to everyone: men and women, rich and poor, young and old.

New Shoes

I love to walk. I love to walk in all seasons, at any time of day, for fun, for fitness, for transportation. I have only one problem with walking: *shoes*. Because my feet are thin and bony, my shoes wear out within six months. I'll find my favourite sports shoes full of holes on the inside! I fix the holes with padded adhesive patches but after a few more months the patches wear away too. So by the end of a year, when blisters appear on my heels, I'm forced to buy another pair. Then, for six months, I enjoy the comfort of new shoes until the cycle starts all over again.

Like most of us, I'm rarely conscious of my shoes – except for the uncomfortable days near the end of their life cycle. However, I often think about the interesting places my shoes take me. Places like the park near my house, part of the huge ravine system that is one of this city's treasures. Places like the farmers' market where we walk and wander on a Saturday morning. Places like the streets in the downtown core where I spend my work days. Whenever I want to rejoice in the beauty of God's creation, all I have to do is look at my shoes and remember.

When I make my annual trip to the sports store for new shoes, I invariably have one uncomfortable moment. Happy as I am to find new shoes that fit and to forget about the blister problem for another few months, I feel a twinge of sadness. That's not because of any sentimental attachment (oh, the memories of the wonderful places we have visited together!) but because my old, worn-out shoes have a new destination.

The managers of the sports store keep a recycling bin handy. They collect their customers' cast-offs and donate them to a downtown shelter for the homeless. Buying my new shoes thus reminds me that I live in a world where my "necessities" are someone else's "luxuries." I have the simple pleasure, not just of wearing new shoes, but of being able to pay for them.

O Lord of those who walk and wander, however little I may have, there are so many others who have less. Teach me to share my bounty.

Hope

A Bunch of Dead Tulips

Clean Pyjamas

The Unknown Shopper

God's Garage Sale

Win, Place and Show

A Better Life

Fridays, 12:15 p.m.

A Bunch of Dead Tulips

The volunteers had set up their displays in the lobby of a mid-town office building. There were posters taped to the walls and brochures spread out on a table, but what really caught my eye were the women holding bunches of tulips in their arms. This was the annual public campaign of the Parkinson Foundation; selling flowers is a standard way to raise funds these days. On a beautiful April day the very idea of tulips attracted a good crowd of supporters. How lovely for a charity to choose an emblem so closely associated with spring.

I handed my money to one of the volunteers and received my bunch of tulips in return. What a disappointment! The tulips seemed almost dead. Perhaps the Foundation had tried to save money by purchasing cheap flowers well past their prime. Never mind, I told myself as I rode the subway home, they might look better in a vase. The important thing was to support this worthy cause.

At home I examined the tulips again. Free from their cellophane wrappings, they looked even worse, wobbling in every direction. Nevertheless it seemed a shame to throw them out immediately. I found a tall vase with a narrow neck, thinking that this shape might offer the most support for the poor flowers. Cutting a few inches off the bottom of the weak stems, I did my best to make some sort of arrangement. It looked pathetic. Oh well, I could always throw them out later, I reasoned, and turned to more pleasant thoughts such as the prospects for dinner.

The next day the tulips looked considerably better: the day after, better still. Was this my imagination? Then I realized that the tulips hadn't been half dead when I brought them home. In fact, they had been so fresh from the greenhouse that they hadn't yet started to open! A few days in a sunny room in a vase full of warm water and presto! Their beauty unfolded right before my eyes. Deep pink streaked with delicate cream on strong straight stems: how had I ever thought these wondrous flowers were dead?

My ignorance concerning tulips, dead or alive, is a poignant mirror of the discrimination that many people still experience today. Some "normal" individuals look at a person with different abilities and see someone who isn't really "alive." They see shaking hands, halting speech; they say, anyone who has to live like that might just as well be "dead."

I obviously know very little about tulips. No matter. But this I do know: my eyes are open to the beauty of those struggling with disabilities. My heart understands the hope that every human being needs. Beauty and hope – so aptly symbolized by tulips in the spring.

O Lord of spring flowers, your message of hope inspires me all year long.

Clean Pyjamas

After six months of tension at work, the flare-up of an old sports injury and a tragic death in the family, David started to unravel. His father noticed it during one of their regular morning telephone calls: David, usually a pillar of strength to everyone around him, sounded strangely agitated about the lamentable state of the world. Then it came out that David had checked all the details of his old insurance policies.

Seriously alarmed by this wild talk, David's father instantly got into his car and drove over to his son's house. What he found was not reassuring: David crying and obviously in crisis. Usually the most abstemious of men, David poured himself a stiff drink (at nine o'clock in the morning!), another sign that something was definitely wrong. When David's younger brother arrived, the concerned relatives called their doctor, who ordered an ambulance and told everyone to stay calm.

The ambulance arrived, and it was the diplomatic brother's job to convince David to cooperate. To everyone's surprise, after the earlier fireworks, David was willing to follow his doctor's orders, but on one condition: he needed a minute or two to shower and change. In spite of frustration and rage, feelings of despair and futility, David refused to go to the hospital unless he could put on a pair of clean pyjamas!

A week later, feeling much calmer thanks to new medication and a helpful psychiatrist, David talked about this humbling experience with his parish priest. The two middle-aged friends shared stories of growing older and feeling out of touch at times; they talked about their doubts and frustrations when hope was absent from their lives; they admitted that sometimes God seemed to be asking too much of them.

By now David could laugh about his trip to the hospital, especially his insistence on taking a shower and changing his clothes. There he was, wishing he were dead and forgotten, yet he took the time to put on clean pyjamas. His friend said one word: "Dignity," and David instantly understood. On that memorable morning, in spite of feeling hopeless and helpless, David still cared enough about himself to be clean and presentable in public.

For a long time after that, David thought about this conversation. The tensions at work had not magically disappeared and the sports injury still needed treatment, but David looked at these problems with new eyes now. Every time he remembered the "clean pyjamas," he grinned. They were a symbol of his faith in himself and his hope for the future. Whatever God sent him, he would do his best to treat himself with love. And dignity.

O Lord the Good Shepherd, as I search for you during my darkest hour, you are there close at hand, ready and waiting to be found.

The Unknown Shopper

The doctor told me to take it easy for a few weeks. No sports, no music, no housework, no writing – all because of a painful problem with my neck. Discouraged by the prospect of a month with nothing to occupy me but a little light office work and regular visits to the physiotherapist, I stopped off at the library for an armload of books. I could at least indulge my love of mysteries without one twinge of guilt: I was only following doctor's orders.

That night I made myself as comfortable as I could, lying on the couch with a flexible ice pack under my neck. I had begun to follow the exploits of a handsome detective in romantic Yorkshire when a small scrap of carefully folded paper fell out of my library book. It didn't look at all familiar. On closer inspection, it turned out to be someone else's shopping list. There in a neat feminine script were the items: diapers, bananas, peas & carrots, Pablum, cookies. A line or two later, perhaps indicating a different store, was a reminder to buy flowers: plumeria and freesias. I put aside my murder mystery and pondered the shopping list instead.

Sherlock Holmes could have deduced quite a bit about the Unknown Shopper from the nine words written on her list. He might begin by saying that she was an organized yet thrifty woman, because she took the time to make a list, using a scrap of paper, not a whole piece, and writing neatly between the lines. She was not too young – her handwriting was mature with no fancy curls or flourishes – but still of child-bearing age. Her baby was at least six months old, since she wanted Pablum and cookies. The woman knew something about flowers (after all, she was looking for plumeria and freesias, not plain old carnations).

Obviously her life was going well: in spite of having a very young child, she still had the time and energy to shop for flowers and read library books. Lastly, she cared about the books she read, using a bookmark, not wantonly turning down the corner of a page to mark her place.

As I pursued my little exercise in deduction, I forgot about my stiff neck. Thank you, Ms. Unknown Shopper, for entering my life on a night when my spirits were low and I needed cheering up. The handsome fictional detective in romantic, far-off Yorkshire just wasn't up to the challenge. You may be a stranger to me, but you are a kindred spirit, part of my community. You not only provided a welcome distraction but your list made me realize that I am not alone. You live in my neighbourhood, shop in the same familiar stores, visit the same library and take time to buy flowers.

By the way, I hope you found the plumeria and freesias.

O Lord of libraries and grocery stores, thank you for the comforting presence of kindred spirits - be they friends or strangers like the Unknown Shopper.

God's Garage Sale

What do you do with your old clothes? The jeans that are too tight, the sweater that shrank in the wash, the shirt that never fit properly even when it was new? Is it hard for you to part with your possessions, even if you no longer want or need them? Do you, like many folks today, have enough relics from the 1960s and '70s to start your own vintage clothing store? Here is one family's solution to the problem.

As far back as I can remember, my family had a specially designated place for old clothes. Dad simply brought home a huge paper rice sack from his store and Mom propped it up in a corner of the cedar closet in the basement. This was our official "poor bag," a name that might not be politically correct today, but was the family shorthand for our ongoing St. Vincent de Paul collection centre. We had a family rule: anything that no longer fit anyone (hand-me-downs were another fact of life) must be promptly relegated to the bag in the basement. When we complained that there were never enough old clothes left over for school plays or Hallowe'en parties, Mom invariably retorted, "It's a sin to keep good things hanging around when someone else could use them." Our closets stayed neat and the old clothes problem was permanently solved.

Ever since, I have tried to pass along my old clothes while they still have some useful life in them. I'll watch the parish bulletin for the announcement about "Bundle Sunday," our regular collection for the St. Vincent de Paul Society.

My used clothes will help the Society with its programs that bring hope to inner-city children, struggling families, single mothers, recovering alcoholics.

In the church parking lot on Bundle Sunday I find a small truck waiting, already half full of plastic bags. A patient volunteer sits in the back of the truck, keeping an eye on the about-to-be recycled possessions of dozens of people. In a few days someone else will be enjoying these treasures.

Why do I never feel the urge to hold a garage sale, selling old clothes and other household junk on my front lawn some Saturday morning? If I did, all I would have to show after a hard day of working in the hot sun would be a little extra money. Instead, I try to continue the family tradition, a cycle of sharing. By supporting Bundle Sunday I keep my closets tidy and let God run the garage sale instead.

O Lord of linen shifts and leather sandals, thank you for silk scarves and faded blue jeans, everything that clothes my body and celebrates my self

Win, Place and Show

My brother Tony was born on a hot August day around lunchtime. By nightfall word had spread through the family: something was wrong at the hospital. The attending pediatrician bluntly told my distraught parents that the baby was "possibly" deaf, blind, mute, retarded. With his thick head of hair and skin discoloured by jaundice, the baby looked very much like a scrawny yellow mouse when he came home from the hospital five days later. My parents put aside the names they had selected over the last few months. Instead they chose "Anthony Joseph," two names with a powerful significance to Italian families, and asked for God's special protection of their youngest child.

Tony was too weak to nurse. Instead, my resourceful mother expressed her own milk, took a baby bottle, enlarged the hole in the nipple, and virtually poured the milk into the little mouth. If the baby managed to take a whole ounce at one feeding, everyone rejoiced. The poor mouse cried a lot and needed round-the-clock attention. But time passed. Eventually we older kids took turns rocking the carriage in the kitchen while Mom cooked dinner. In spite of the doctor's dire predictions, our family saw no signs of blindness, mental limitations, or deafness. Tony was far from mute: he talked a blue streak. New specialists had a more positive approach to the very rare condition with the long funny name. In time Tony grew into a thoughtful, bright and unfailingly kind child.

More time passed. Tony went to good schools; took part in a third-year-abroad program at a famous university; did student volunteer work in Europe; went to an even more famous university for graduate studies. Who cares about wearing a hearing aid, and "rare medical conditions," when you have a fine memory and the capacity for hard work?

No longer sickly and weak, Tony was now as strong as a horse: a racehorse to be exact, just like the horses in a racing stable he loved to visit during his summer holidays. The once- frail child had become a strong, well-groomed adult, a natural athlete who participated in hundreds of road races, including half a dozen marathons. Tony ran in Cape Cod, cycled through France, hiked in the Rockies, skied in glamorous Alpine resorts, a far cry from the little baby who was once too weak to nurse.

Tony recently bought a condominium on a quiet midtown street, thrilled by the location of the new building. One of the city's most delightful fitness trails passes right behind the complex. Tony can run for miles along the wooded path, then enjoy a shower and whirlpool afterward in the apartment's relaxing spa. This remarkable person, an inspiring symbol of hope, has never, not once in 38 years, complained about the rare condition with the long funny name. If Life were a horse race, you couldn't back a finer human being than a winner like my brother Tony, with legs like a racehorse and a heart of solid gold.

O L1mord, you gave sight to the blind and opened the mouths of those who could not speak. I always wanted a little brother. Thanks for sending Tony.

A Better Life

Rocco left his small town in Southern Italy in 1901. His mother was a widow and they were desperately poor: family allowances and other government benefits didn't exist back then, so with his mother's blessing Rocco decided to look for a better life elsewhere. He could not read, nor could he write, but arriving in Toronto he found work almost immediately as a simple labourer. After three years, Rocco had saved enough money to bring his mother, his young wife Caterina and their little son Salvatore from the old country. Eventually they bought a tiny house, exactly 11 feet wide, on a street with other immigrant families in the oldest part of the city. Luck was with him from the beginning, because his "pick and shovel" job with the city was secure, and even in the bleakness of the Great Depression, he always had work.

Caterina was as industrious as her husband. She made her own soap over a fire in the backyard, preserved dandelion greens layered with salt in earthenware crocks, wrapped hot bricks in newspaper to keep the beds warm on the cold winter nights, cooked for the growing family, and still found time to go to church every day. Rocco rented an allotment garden on the edge of the city, and his fresh tomatoes and peppers were a welcome addition to the dinner table during the summer. In the tiny house, the family, now consisting of parents, grandmother and eight children, flourished. Caterina and Rocco never did learn to read and write.

Today their descendants include university professors, engineers, teachers, economists, secretaries, nurses, lawyers, business men and women, plumbing contractors, computer scientists, skilled tradesmen, accountants, people who sit on the boards of prominent arts organizations, go to the opera, the symphony, the museum. Everyone over the age of seven can read and write.

You can change the names of the characters in this true story. I have called them "Nana and Papa" all my life but you might prefer "Olga and Kasimir" or "Marie-Claire and Jean-Baptiste" or "Brigid and Sean" or "Benazir and Gurdip" or "Selena and José" or "Liu and Chung." The names might be different but the story remains the same: immigrants come here to find a better life, if not for themselves, then ultimately for their families.

Caterina and Rocco have been buried for many years in a cemetery called, fittingly enough, "Mount Hope." They left their home in the old country inspired by hope, sustained by faith in themselves, the future, their God. Today their descendants remember with love those two people whose courage and perseverance gave all of us a better life.

O Lord of immigrants and wayfarers, many of our grandparents looked for a better life in a new world. May we appreciate this great nation they built from sea to sea.

Fridays, 12:15 p.m.

A hot Friday in June. Quite by chance, it was 1:15 p.m. when I walked by a church near the office. People of all ages, shapes and sizes suddenly streamed from the doors leading to the parish hall – perhaps 30 laughing, joking individuals. They carried paper cups, presumably of coffee or tea; many lit cigarettes as soon as they were safely out-of-doors.

A young woman, hardly more than a teenager, wore a smart slipdress with a contrasting T-shirt underneath. Her older companion, wearing a blue batik jumper, might have been a retired teacher. Another woman, with silver streaks in her well-groomed hair, sported a white linen jacket. One equally handsome older man had his long grey hair tied back in a ponytail.

I kept watching. A young guy in a madras shirt and khaki shorts looked like a visitor to a summer resort. There were baseball caps and straw hats, peasant blouses and work shirts, gym bags, backpacks and smart leather totes. Three older men, perhaps retired truckers or construction workers with strong, sinewy forearms, stood under a tree talking earnestly. A postman, movie-star handsome with wrap-around sunglasses and a deep bronze tan, held his mail bag tucked under one arm.

Whatever could this motley crew be doing together in a church basement at lunchtime on Friday? Who would plan a meeting at noon and reasonably expect to have this kind of attendance? Alcoholics Anonymous, that's who. There on the handle of the door hung a hand-written cardboard sign, with the famous letters "AA" inscribed on it.

In the interests of anonymity, someone quickly removed the sign as the members flooded onto the sidewalk. Without spotting those tell-tale letters, I might have speculated forever on the nature of the group or the purpose of the meeting. And why? Because not one of those people smoking cigarettes and drinking coffee looked even remotely like "someone with a drinking problem."

I sat down on the curb to watch this scene from a discreet distance. When Bill W. and Dr. Bob, the founders of AA, held their first meeting in 1935, this must have been their dream: people from all walks of life joined together anonymously, giving each other support through the common experience of addiction and recovery, sustained by their belief that Someone greater than themselves would help them, one day at a time. Every AA group is a tribute to the power of that belief.

I was deeply moved. My own childhood was scarred by my dear father's occasional descents into an alcoholic hell. Thank you, AA group, Fridays at 12:15 p.m., for sharing your hope with someone who just happened to be standing across the street an hour later.

O Lord who blessed the wine at the marriage feast of Cana, help those escaping from the despair of addiction into the recovery of hope.

Joy

Tranquilitas

At the concert, the conductor turned to face the audience and announced, "This motet is a remarkable portrayal of an episode in the life of Jesus." He then explained how the composer had described in music the famous incident when Jesus fell asleep on board a boat, only to be awakened by the cries of the frightened disciples. The motet vividly portrayed the gathering storm, the terror of the apostles, and finally the calming of the waves and the restoration of peace to the sea.

Learning the unaccompanied motet had been a challenge during our week of rehearsals. We may have been experienced amateur singers, yet we doubted our ability to master the complexities of this piece. In fact, we altos had been in trouble ever since the first rehearsal. The opening bars were the worst! The conductor reassured us that an organist would play those tricky first notes as a reminder on the night of the concert. Nevertheless, I diligently practised the difficult opening at every opportunity, especially in the privacy of my morning shower.

On the night of the performance, we successfully navigated the hazard of the opening; the different voices entered in turn, and the storm began to gather. Wave upon wave of musical phrases piled up; the terrified disciples raised their voices in agitation, crying, "Save us, Lord," in Latin of course, and Jesus uttered his memorable words, "Why are you worried,

O ye of little faith?" With growing assurance as the music swept us along, our voices sailed confidently through the sea of notes.

Jesus stood in the bow of the boat, stretching his arm over the waves, and a miracle happened: the waves receded and the sea was calm again. We, too, sang a miracle. The musical intensity dropped, as the waves in the Sea of Galilee once dropped. Those of us who had experienced fear in the face of impending musical disaster had come through the storm. While singing about the miracle that had calmed the disciples' fears, our own fears had likewise been calmed by the conductor's confidence in our ability to learn this difficult work.

Eventually we arrived at the resolution and peace of the conclusion, finishing on a note of tranquillity. We sang the very last word, *tranquilitas,* over and over again, the repetitions like waves flowing endlessly to a distant shore. The music summed up the human yearning for peace and order, the calm we miss in the stress and struggle of everyday life. Calm and peace: there it was, easily within our grasp, just as the conductor had insisted. Like the disciples in the boat with Jesus long ago, our evening was finally blessed with a memorable experience of contentment: true tranquillity.

O Lord who calmed the waves of the sea, you stand amongst us in every kind of weather, pointing the way to true tranquillity and peace.

My First Moose

Until recently I had never seen a moose. During all my years of camping, hiking, canoeing, exploring, I had never been in the right place at the right time to see this typically Canadian resident of the northern woods. Porcupine, deer, wolves: yes. Elk, big-horn sheep, coyote: yes. Moose: no.

In fact, it became a family joke. Auntie Bertha had spent hundreds of nights sleeping out-of-doors in her tent, suffering millions of mosquito bites and assorted other discomforts; she had spent hours hiking in the bush and canoeing in the wilderness, but she had never seen a moose! My nieces and nephews saw moose (plural) during their summers at camp; visiting relatives from up north casually encountered them on the highway. But I had always drawn a blank in the moose-sighting sweepstakes.

Over the years I had witnessed many of nature's other glories: the immense rafts of birds darkening the sky at Point Pelee in the spring migration; millions of monarch butterflies decorating the trees like so many living Christmas ornaments in the fall. My memory's personal wildlife documentary holds some remarkable sights: rare whooping cranes splashing through the marshes in their winter home in Texas; enormous grey whales nuzzling their equally enormous young in the warm, salty waters of Scammon's Lagoon in Mexico. For heaven's sake, a sleek young fox regularly sauntered through our backyard in mid-town Toronto! But I had never seen a moose.

Then, one grey afternoon in November, as we were leaving Algonquin Park in the fading daylight, a huge bull moose appeared on the deserted highway in front of our car. Screeching to a sudden stop, we pulled onto the shoulder and watched this giant of the forest lumber across the road, taking his own sweet time and giving us an unexpected opportunity to enjoy the spectacle. Then Mr. Moose calmly re-entered the woods and disappeared.

Needless to say, I went wild. The next day, I bought assorted souvenir postcards, all featuring moose in different poses, reserving a few for the nieces and nephews who had heartlessly teased me about the "dozens" they saw every year at camp. For the next two days, I told everyone we met: our hostess at the farmhouse bed-and-breakfast, the waiter at the lakeside restaurant.

Back home, I put a moose magnet up on the fridge. My magnet is more than a tribute to my first moose. It reminds me that we can never plan our peak moments of joy. They come as an unexpected gift from the mysterious and playful God of Surprises.

O Lord of the wilderness, bless every living creature here with me as I pray in the cathedral of the forest.

"Wait Until You Get to Paradise!"

The telephone roused me from a sound sleep, but after a few words from the overseas operator I sat up, fully awake. The collect call came from Rome. Members of my family had been involved in a serious car accident just a few miles from the airport. Instead of sitting comfortably on an airplane heading back home to Toronto, they were now in hospital thousands of miles away.

For the rest of the day the nightmare continued. I had to break the bad news to other family members, inform the airline, contact our insurance agent. By late afternoon I was exhausted. A nap proved useless: I was too tired to sleep. A hard work-out at the gym barely took the edge off my anxiety. Dinner was a disaster. How could I enjoy my meal when assorted loved ones now suffered so far away from home?

Finally, I retreated upstairs with a book. For months I had been slowly making my way through the cantos of the *Divine Comedy* and now I was nearly finished. I had travelled with Dante through the many levels of the Inferno, met the doomed lovers Paolo and Francesca, shuddered at the gruesome death of the wicked Count Ugolino, listened to the elegiac lament of the once-great Ulysses. Eventually I had landed on the hopeful shores of Purgatory and now I soared with Dante on his ascent into Paradise.

My brother Tony had urged me on during this epic journey; his words of encouragement now sang in my ears: *Wait until you get to Paradise.* Various relatives might be stuck in the Hell of a Roman hospital, but for an hour or two I could be with Dante in Heaven.

To help my concentration, I read the last six cantos aloud. Worn out from the events of the day, I was more receptive to the poetry than ever before. As we approached the climax – Dante's vision of the ecstasy of Paradise – tears welled up in my tired eyes. I kept reading out loud, startled by Dante's sudden humility (he had been a proud, stiff-necked guide through the rest of our journey together), overwhelmed by the majestic simplicity of his conception of Heaven.

Here were the souls of the blessed, arranged like the petals of a vast celestial rose around the figure of the triumphant Christ, unbearably beautiful to contemplate. Surrendering to this vision of Eternal Bliss, I eventually lost myself in a mystical dream of transcending joy. I could hardly see the words on the page through my tears.

Years have passed since the disaster on the road to the Rome airport; the details have faded in my memory. The compassionate hospital clerk who spoke to me twice a day? The friendly insurance adjuster? The concerned travel agent? I no longer remember the names of these kind, helpful people. But my journey with Dante is impossible to forget.

O Lord of mystics and poets, in life as in literature, I can hardly wait until I get to Paradise.

Mirror, Mirror

When I caught her reflection in the mirror, she was sitting on a bench at the gym, holding a pair of ten-pound dumbbells. Tough-looking fitness buffs milled around in the background. The stranger started her routine: standard biceps curls. She wore gloves on her hands and a determined expression on her face. A no-nonsense personal trainer stood off to one side, counting, occasionally offering a word of encouragement or advice. Finally the set of exercises was over. The face of the stranger in the mirror suddenly relaxed and smiled, becoming someone I knew after all: me.

Over the past 18 months, I have become this stranger, thanks to Ana, my trainer at the gym, and her weekly regime of blood, sweat and tears. Well, maybe not exactly blood. Definitely sweat. And since I have cried more than once from terror, exertion and joy, all rolled into one, there have certainly been tears. Ana has changed the way I see my body. Please note: Ana is not a magician. My hair is greyer than it was 18 months ago, the laugh lines on my face deeper and harder to ignore. I am the same quiet introvert who works in offices, studies music and writes books. But training with this gifted professional has taught me something new about perseverance, about faith, but mostly about joy.

Joy? Since I started my weight training as an absolute beginner, the first month was a challenge. Challenge? Sheer torture is a better description. My heart and legs were already strong – I could walk or hike for hours – but my upper body "needed work," as Ana bluntly told me. Muscles that had slumbered in happy neglect for 48 years suddenly woke up, screaming in protest. Furthermore, I was painfully shy around the others at the gym, men and women with sleek bodies and confident demeanour. But my commitment to a year with a personal trainer gave me time to learn, to grow, to change. Soon enough the joy followed.

Joy? The joy of learning, of course. I now understand how to exercise my whole body safely and effectively, even calling the muscles by their correct names. The joy of accomplishment. Today I laugh off dozens of push-ups when I could barely manage one or two before. The joy of friendship. Ana and I chatter away happily during my workouts; I give her cooking tips and she tells me about the celebrities spotted at the gym. The joy of improved fitness. After six months of weight training, my camping equipment wasn't heavy anymore. The joy of beauty. Oh the pleasure of seeing the definition in my back and shoulders, thanks to all those exercises for front and rear deltoids!

Best of all is the joy that comes from discovering new possibilities for the same old body, the "temple of the Holy Spirit" which has been entrusted to my care.

O Lord of power and might, you have given me this body, as well as my soul and my mind. Teach me to appreciate these changing, surprising gifts.

Our Daily Bread

I could write a whole book about the joy I have experienced over a lifetime of eating. But how would I limit myself to a manageable number of memories? I would have to include the special Mello-roll ice cream cones from my childhood. One perfectly ripe pear served with rich Gorgonzola cheese, a memorable dessert enjoyed in Italy many years ago. My mother's spaghetti sauce (the younger generation of our family calls it "liquid gold"). Auntie Ruby's butter tarts. The veal stew with dumplings in a rural Connecticut inn. The fresh-from-the-oven bread at the bakery near Nana's house. Grannie's famous banana cake.

I am annoyed by restaurant reviewers who describe some special dish as "decadent" or "wicked" or "sinful." This overused shorthand for "superbly delicious" runs contrary to what I have experienced of the pleasures of the table. Far from being sinful, eating is a perfect opportunity to experience God's gracious concern for our health and happiness three times a day. We need to eat to live, yet what a wealth of simple pleasures is found in food: not an enemy but a friend to nourish and sustain us, body and soul, day after day after day!

"O taste and see the goodness of the Lord," urges the writer of Psalm 34. In just such a spirit I turn to my kitchen notebook for the recipe for Scripture Cake, a family tradition at Easter time. This spicy concoction uses milk, honey, raisins, figs, dates, almonds: every one of its ingredients mentioned specifically somewhere in the Bible. The very old recipe was originally fashioned as a puzzle ("Take 2 cups of Jeremiah 6:20") to help young chefs learn their way around the scriptures. Such a recipe is also a "superbly delicious" reminder of the everyday blessings of food, part of the history of our salvation from earliest times.

Last night, relatives from South America joined us for pasta, roast beef, salad, apple pie – a family-style dinner in the backyard. Tonight for dinner we are having leftovers. Jesus taught us to say, "Give us this day our daily bread." I would also add, "Bless us, O Lord, and these thy gifts – leftover pasta, roast beef, salad, apple pie – and happy are we who are called to your supper."

O Lord, you invite me to a heavenly banquet; thank you for the preview here on earth.

Happy Families

I was visiting the famous art gallery in Florence, as tourists on vacation often do. Guidebook in hand, I moved from room to room, stopping to look here and there, referring every now and then to the printed page for information and direction. I turned a corner to enter yet another room, and came to a sudden stop. One small, round painting, a recently cleaned masterpiece, took me by surprise!

It was a painting of the Holy Family: three easily recognizable human beings, a mother, father and child. Their skin tones were especially fresh, the faces realistic. Here were three real-life participants in the ongoing human drama known as "family," not ethereal beings temporarily visiting from another dimension of time and space. Joseph in the background looked just like one of my uncles; Mary lifted strong, shapely arms above her head to hold the infant Jesus. His chubby fingers were curled in the braids of his mother's hair, just like real babies do today. And the colours: bright, clear red, blue, gold; no dull grey or brown for these people. Here was life, here was joy, here was a family, happy to be together.

Why did I feel such a surge of joy on first encountering this famous painting? Because I was in the presence of an undisputed masterpiece by one of the greatest artists of all time? Perhaps in part. But I remember my explanation to friends when they noticed the tears starting in my eyes. I said in a hushed tone, "But they look so alive!" They lived through the painting on the wall, but not because the artist had engaged in any tricks of magic realism, creating something that cleverly mimicked a photograph. No, these people were alive because it was this artist's special genius to capture the force and energy of human life at its grandest. Jesus, Mary and Joseph looked just like us: living, breathing members of the human family at its best.

I have plenty of opportunities to see paintings, listen to hymns and hear sermons that stress the pale, other-worldly goodness of this one Family, usually dignified with the adjective "Holy." Some artists, musicians or preachers feel that it is their duty to remind the rest of us lowly sinners of the remote perfection of Jesus, Mary and Joseph. During the time that I stood in the gallery overcome by joy, I looked instead at a family that was also completely familiar, with shapely, strong arms and rich, full lips, dressed in gloriously bright colours; smiling at me with human, not transcendental, joy. I hope I remembered to smile back.

O Lord of cousins and in-laws, I am grateful for the genius of artists: they remind me that your holy family shared human smiles with one another.

Let There Be Light

It was Holy Thursday evening. My walk to church took me past the entrance to an attractive park, the ravine home of many birds and animals, including a family of foxes. Well after dark, no wildlife would be visible, yet someone was staring intently into the distance through a pair of binoculars. Why? It was far too late for bird watching and the foxes stayed carefully hidden when there were people nearby. Then the light dawned on me. The silent watcher on the edge of the ravine was looking at a comet! I timidly asked if I too might have a peek. The amateur astronomer eagerly shared her binoculars and thus I had my first view of Hale-Bopp. The comet with the spectacular tail hovered low in the northwest sky, a heavenly spectacle visible for several weeks in the spring of 1997.

Soon enough I had to leave the ravine look-out and continue on my way to church. The Holy Thursday liturgy unfolded in all its graceful beauty. When Mass was over, I walked home. By then, the comet had disappeared, but now I knew where in the sky to look on subsequent clear evenings throughout the spring.

The next day was the sombre solemnity of Good Friday. Then came Holy Saturday night and time for the Easter Vigil. Back to church I went yet again, this time all dressed up. It was my turn to be a lector, so in a smart new suit and decent shoes, I took the car instead of walking. I couldn't see the entrance to the ravine. Was my comet-watching friend out again tonight? Driving in my car I couldn't tell.

The church was completely dark when I arrived. We the lectors took our stations in various places, reading lamps spilling small pools of light onto our lecterns. The majestic liturgy began; our fellow parishioners listened in the darkness. Those watching for comets outside might admire the flash of light blazing across the northwest sky; the lectors indoors read the story of an even more glorious display of celestial fireworks.

In the beginning, the story told us, there was only a formless, desolate void of nothingness. Someone decided to fill this great emptiness with animals and plants, a man and a woman, a wealth of living creatures created in love to live in peace and harmony. But before there could be birds in the sky or foxes in the ravines, even the Creator had to begin at the beginning. The spirit of God, moving over the waters of darkness, uttered one famous command. All of us listening in the darkened church heard the words that brought back to me the memory of Holy Thursday night and the brilliant beauty of the comet: "And so God commanded, 'Let there be light.' And light appeared."

O Lord of eternal light, the signs of your presence are always with me: from foxes living in ravines to comets blazing across the sky.